NEVER TOO OLD

To: MARK & SUSAN
Blessings on ya
Pastor Mel
(Heb 4:12)

NEVER TOO OLD
GOD ISN'T FINISHED WITH ME YET!

The Faithful Life and Legacy of Mel Sumrall
Founder of Denton Bible Church

CONNIE COHN

XULON PRESS

Xulon Press
2301 Lucien Way #415
Maitland, FL 32751
407.339.4217
www.xulonpress.com

Unless otherwise indicated, scripture quotations are taken from The New American Standard Bible (NASB). Copyright © 1960, 1962, 1963, 1968, 1971, 1972, 1973, 1975, 1977, 1995 by The Lockman Foundation;

Unless otherwise indicated, scripture quotations are taken from The New International Version (NIV). Copyright © 1973, 1978, 1984, 2011 by Biblica, Inc.™. Used by permission. All rights reserved.

Printed in the United States of America.

ISBN-13: 9781545641361

Endorsements

Few are those who become heroes while they are still alive. Mel is a spiritual hero to so many people because of what he allowed God to do in him and through him. What I like best about this book is that those who know Mel Sumrall the best, love and respect him most. His life, his marriage, his ministry, and his heart to take the Gospel of Jesus Christ to the world are all models for any who will stop, read, and listen to this powerful example.

Mark L. Bailey
President
Dallas Theological Seminary

I met Mel Sumrall when we attended Dallas Theological Seminary together. He had a passion to follow God with all his heart, and that passion continues today. God has used him to not only found Denton Bible Church, but to also take the gospel around the world. Mel Sumrall's story will inspire and motivate you to follow his example of attempting great things for God.

Dr. Tony Evans
Pastor, Oak Cliff Bible Fellowship

I can identify with Mel Sumrall's story. Though he states my own influence in his life, particularly regarding the "One Another" concepts in Scripture, he has been an encouragement to me as well–and his story explains why! I recommend this book. You'll be blessed.

Dr. Gene A. Getz
Professor, Pastor, Author

As a young faculty member at DTS when Mel arrived as a student, I was impressed by Mel's life story. His faith and commitment to our Lord were inspiring. Later I met disciples of the ministry in Europe after the fall of Communism. We often met ministering and making disciples in young churches. I know if you read Mel's story God can use it in your life to become a disciple of our Lord.

Dr. Elliott Johnson
Professor, Dallas Theological Seminary

Author's Note

It has been a joy and a privilege to write the amazing story of Pastor Mel Sumrall. Mel came from humble beginnings as did Denton Bible Church. My late husband, Steve, and I came to Denton Bible Church in July 2009. To have been at DBC from its earliest days would have been heaven, but writing this book has been the next best thing.

Thanks to everyone who made time to be interviewed. Your stories helped paint a picture of who Mel is and the incredible impact he has had on so many lives. The stories in the book represent a small fraction of the lives that Mel has touched. Mel and I both desired to include more stories, but we had to stop somewhere.

I have verified facts, dates, and events to the best of my ability. If there are errors, I take full responsibility.

Connie Cohn

Dedication

Mel

First, I dedicate this book to Almighty God who made everything in this book possible. Next, I dedicate this book to Patty, my sweetheart of seventy years and ten months, and to our children, Susan, Jerry, Karen, Laura, and Pamela (deceased). Finally, I dedicate this book to Pastor Tom, the former and present staff, and the people of Denton Bible Church.

Connie

I dedicate this book to my heavenly Father who rescued me out of deep darkness and despair in 1979 and brought me into His marvelous light through Jesus Christ, my precious Lord and Savior. Now, thirty-nine years later, He has filled my heart with unspeakable love, joy and peace. To Him be glory forever and ever!

He lifted me out of the slimy pit,
out of the mud and mire;
He set my feet on a rock
and gave me a firm place to stand.
He put a new song in my mouth,
a hymn of praise to our God.
Many will see and fear the LORD
and put their trust in Him.

Psalm 40:2-3

I also dedicate this book to Jacob, my firstborn grandson. You bring me much joy, and I cherish the memories we've made together. I look forward to many more treasured times together, my sweet Jacob. I love you!

Acknowledgements

A part from Christ I can do nothing – literally! He has been my constant source of strength throughout the writing process. I praise Him and thank Him for His love, mercy and grace in bringing this book to fruition.

Many people have helped in my journey toward getting this book published. This book would not have been published without the encouragement of Margaret Ashmore, a dear sister in Christ. When I presented her with the idea, she said, "Go for it. Mel's story needs to be told." Margaret has been a constant source of support throughout the writing process. Thank you, sweet Margaret!

Thanks to Shannon and Donna Irving and Vonnie George who believed in this project enough to help me financially towards the cost of publishing the book. Thank you, Shannon, for helping me prepare the manuscript and pictures to submit to the publisher. You have been a blessing throughout the writing process with your technological expertise!

Thanks to Sonjia Bradshaw for her many hours work editing the book. It has been a joy getting to know you, Sonjia!

Thanks to John Brown for reading the manuscript and making valuable suggestions.

My pastor, Tommy Nelson, has been an encouragement as he made time for me to interview him and gave me access to wonderful memories of Mel and the founding of Denton Bible Church. Thank you, Tommy, for getting behind this project. Thanks also to Lynn Davenport, Tommy's assistant, for her patience and help with questions I asked and resources I needed for this book. Thanks also to the rest of the DBC staff who have helped in various ways.

Thanks to Ann Little, my mentor and dear friend, who has prayed for me along with a dedicated group of women. Thank you for hosting our prayer times at your home and for the delicious meals you provided.

Thanks to Angie and Bekah Guess for their many hours of work categorizing and putting the pictures online.

The material for the early years of Mel and Patty's life came mainly from the DVD, *The Life of Melvin & Patricia Sumrall*, produced by ngvideoproductions in 2011. This was an invaluable resource that recorded Mel and Patty's memories before Patty succumbed to Alzheimer's.

Thanks to Gaby Ethington for taking much needed photos.

Thanks to my precious brothers and sisters in Christ at Denton Bible Church who have loved me and helped me grow in Christ, especially my Sweat Team family and my *One Anothers* family. Thank you for your excitement over this book being published. I love you all!

Thanks to all the people I interviewed for the book. It has been a delight to hear your stories and marvel at how God intersected your lives with Mel for His kingdom purposes.

Thanks to Dale and Allison, my son and daughter-in-law, and my three grandkids, Jacob, Josh, and Joy, for providing me with joyful times when I needed a break from writing. I love you!

Thanks to everyone at Xulon Press, especially Wallayna Bradford, for their excellent advice and help along the way.

Finally, thanks to Mel Sumrall for loving God with all his heart, mind, soul and strength, and for dedicating his life to serving God these many long years. Thank you, Mel, for your outstanding example of how to love people well yet challenge them to attempt great things for God. You have become a father to me as we have spent this past year working on the book. I love you!

Foreword

I met this remarkable man by God's providence in 1977, and since then Mel and I have been of one mind, in ministry and in life. His wife Patty was the best of encouragers until she went home to be with Christ; Mel has been my constant encourager for over forty years. He runs as diligently at ninety–two as he ran at fifty–two.

This book by Connie Cohn will bless any man or woman who wants to run with God all the way to the end and especially anyone who decides mid-life to begin serving God anew. It will also be a blessing to anyone who has had to overcome difficulties and pain in life and yet must continue.

Mel has been a fine son, Marine, superintendent, student, pastor, and missionary. Churches from Denton to Nepal owe their existence to him. I owe him the greater part of my life as my friend and mentor.

Tommy Nelson
Senior Pastor
Denton Bible Church

Table of Contents

Introduction

The righteous will flourish like a palm tree, they will grow like a cedar of Lebanon; planted in the house of the LORD, they will flourish in the courts of our God. **They will still bear fruit in old age, they will stay fresh and green**, proclaiming, "The LORD is upright; he is my Rock, and there is no wickedness in him." Psalm 92:12–15

Mel Sumrall, at age ninety–two, still produces fruit. He is vigorous, or as the New American Standard translation puts it, "full of sap and very green." Zeal for the Lord's work pulses through Mel's veins and fills him with vitality that is felt in his hugs, heard in his teaching, and seen in his service. Currently, he disciples several men every week, instilling in them his passion to train pastors globally since many foreign pastors have no one to teach them the Bible. He offers a leadership class for young men in their twenties. He leads a class on heaven for widowers and widows. Mel planted a church when he was eighty-four years old.

Age has never held Mel back. He was the oldest student to enroll at Dallas Theological Seminary (DTS) in 1973 at forty-eight years of age, He graduated in the 1976–77 class with a Master of Theology. The Lord called Mel to found Denton Bible Church in 1976 while in his senior year at DTS. From its humble beginning with a handful of people, Denton Bible Church has grown to a congregation of four thousand people over the past forty-two years. About a year after the founding of Denton Bible Church, God brought Tommy Nelson to serve with Mel. The Lord has used these two men to impact His kingdom, not only in Denton, Texas, but around the world.

Tommy took over the leadership of Denton Bible Church when Mel stepped down from pastoring at age sixty-two. But Mel knew his work for the Lord wasn't over. Through a series of events, he joined CRU (formerly Campus Crusade for Christ) and began training pastors around the world. He and his sweetheart Patty, wife of seventy years, taught all over the world for the next thirteen years until Patty, at age seventy-five, could no longer travel because of health issues. Mel has served continuously since then and still pulls in the harness at age ninety-two.

Anyone who spends time with Mel develops fierce loyalty to him. He is a living treasure still dispensing wisdom wrapped in the love of Christ. Mel prays Psalm 71:18-19, "Now that I am old, and my hair is gray, don't leave me, God. I must tell the next generation about Your power and greatness. God, Your goodness reaches far above the skies. You have done wonderful things. God, there is no one like You."

The younger generation hears about God's power and greatness in Mel's leadership class for millennials. Mel is grateful for the opportunity to pour into the lives of these young men. He prays that more "gray heads" will step up and come alongside young people, training them and sending them forth. They are our future. Proverbs 20:29 says that the gray hair of experience is the splendor of the old. Job 12:12 tells us that wisdom belongs to the aged and understanding to the old. Some things can only be learned by living life for a long time. Older people have much to teach the younger generation. Yet many churches today push older people aside while attempting to appeal to the young. The American culture is geared toward youth, and sadly, churches often are too. These congregations lose the wisdom and experience that come with age.

Mel hopes that in telling his story churches and the younger generation will be encouraged once again to look to the older generation as a valuable resource. Mel also wants to challenge older Christians to do what he has done—attempt great things for God, despite age.

Chapter 1

The Early Years

"For we brought nothing into the world, and we can take nothing out of it. But if we have food and clothing, we will be content with that." (First Timothy 6:7–8).

Melvin Luther Sumrall was born into poverty but destined for riches that the world can't offer. Through the hard times in his youth, he learned contentment and so much more. Jerry Wilson Sumrall and Amanda Tidwell Sumrall welcomed Mel into the world on September 21, 1925. Mel was named after his great-grandfather, Martin Luther Sumrall. The Sumrall family migrated from Mississippi where it is believed a logging town is named Sumrall. The Sumrall name comes from the isle of Wight, off Portsmouth, England.

At the time of Mel's birth, Jerry and Amanda lived in Weinert, Texas, located in the Panhandle. In the months that followed, his family moved to Ennis, Texas. Mel's birth, sandwiched between the end of World War I and the beginning of the Great Depression, came at a difficult time in history. His parents had only a fourth-grade education. As often happened at that time, they left school to help support their families.

Jerry and Amanda married when she was sixteen years old. Amanda's mother died when she was young, and she helped care for her younger brothers and sisters until her own marriage. As Mel grew up, he saw his parents' loving marriage relationship. Years later Mel modeled that same love when he married his beloved Patty. Mel had two sisters and a brother. Myrtle, the oldest lived to be ninety-eight. Odetta, next in line, died at the young age of about thirty-five. Jerry, named after his dad, was the third child born to the Sumralls. He died in 2008 at eighty-two years old. Mel was the baby of the family.

During the Depression, Jerry couldn't find work. The family lived in abandoned houses that the city condemned because of toxic well water. Since the only water source was the well, that is what the Sumrall family drank. These abandoned houses not only lacked running water, but also electricity, heat, and telephones. As the Depression dragged on, Mel's shoes wore out. The soles flapped when he walked, and his dad tied them together with copper wire. Amanda used an old Singer sewing machine to make clothes for the kids, including bib overalls and shirts for the boys. The Sumrall family had an ice box like everyone else in those days. They put a sign in the window for the iceman when they needed ice. He would stop his horse, unload the ice from his wagon, bring it in the house, and put it in the ice box. People usually bought 25, 50, or 100 pounds of ice. As head of the family, Jerry sat at the kitchen table and wept because he could not find work to provide for his wife and kids. Feeling desperate and overwhelmed, Jerry searched for some way to make money. Mel shared his father's feelings of despair as he watched him weep.

Jerry helped hungry strangers despite having difficulty feeding his family. Often Mel heard a knock at the back door while the family sat at the dinner table. Mel remembers a typical conversation.

"I haven't had anything to eat for several days," a man said. "If you could give me a little something to eat, I'd be glad to work for you."

His dad replied, "We don't have much, but we're glad to share whatever we have."

Most meals consisted of biscuits or cornbread, beans and gravy. Occasionally, Amanda managed to raise a few chickens, so the family had a bite of meat to eat with their meals. Living through the Great Depression and enduring harsh conditions left Mel with the drive to work hard and succeed. He heard stories of millionaires who jumped out windows when the stock market crashed in 1929. One day they had great wealth and the next day had nothing. In 1933 at the height of the Depression, approximately twenty-five percent of the one hundred twenty-five million people living in the United States were out of work.[1]

During the darkest times, God often brings hope and light. Mel and his family normally attended a Nazarene church, but one evening in 1933 Mel and his brother Jerry asked if they could go to the Baptist church. His parents agreed. Mel heard the good news that Jesus Christ died for his sins and rose again on the third day. The teacher asked if anyone wanted to invite Jesus into their hearts. Mel raised his hand, prayed to receive Christ, and was baptized that same night. Although Mel was now a child of God, it would be years before anyone discipled him. Sadly, not much spiritual growth took place until God intervened in a dramatic fashion years later.

Despite the harsh conditions, children found ways to have fun. Most boys played marbles, and by the fourth grade Mel was champion at his school. When the boys played, the winner took all the marbles. One day, Mel's pockets bulged with all his winnings. He entered the auditorium, which had a concrete floor, and as Mel leaned back in his seat, the marbles started rolling out of his pockets, making a huge noise. In addition to marbles, kids also played tops. The cylinders with a pointed end had a string wrapped around it, and Mel grew quite skilled at throwing his top on the ground and watching it spin.

Mel was ten years old when his mother was diagnosed with tuberculosis. The doctor prescribed the standard treatment: move to a climate with clean, dry air. Jerry's brother, Frank, lived in Pueblo, Colorado, so Mel's folks decided to move the family to Pueblo. Since Jerry and Amanda didn't have a car, Frank, along with his little son Sam, drove to Ennis to pick them up in his Model A. The car had a single seat for passengers as well as a rumble seat, an upholstered exterior seat that folded into the rear of early automobiles. Jerry built a wooden platform for Mel and his brother Jerry and cousin Sam to sit on for the drive to Pueblo.

The move to Colorado took place during the Dust Bowl. The 1934 *Yearbook of Agriculture*, produced by the US Department of Agriculture stated, "Approximately thirty-five million acres of formerly cultivated land have essentially been destroyed for crop production. One hundred million acres now in crops have lost all, or most, of the topsoil. One hundred twenty-five million acres of land now in crops are rapidly losing topsoil."[2]

Thick dust obscured everything. As the kids rode on the platform outside the car, the dust choked them, making it hard to breathe in spite of cloths covering their faces. The Model A chugged along at twenty-five miles an hour for the seven hundred and twelve-mile trip. The Sumrall family endured the harsh conditions and arrived safely in Pueblo where Mel attended Fountain Grade School from fourth through sixth grade.

Mel was twelve years old the summer he played fast pitch softball with the city's league. One day, he played several games one after another. Afterwards, his muscles ached, and Mel came to his father. "Dad, my legs hurt."

Jerry nodded toward the road, "Walk downtown with me." He figured Mel would walk off the soreness. Instead, Mel sagged against his Dad, unable to walk without support. Jerry immediately took Mel to see Dr. Wade. With his knees tied to his chest, Mel endured the pain of a spinal tap. The results came back—polio, the same strain as President Franklin Roosevelt. A polio epidemic swept the country that summer. Dr. Jonas Salk's development of the polio vaccine would come too late for Mel and countless other children. Swimming pools, movie houses, and public gatherings shut down to stop the spread of the highly contagious disease. The Sumrall house was quarantined. No one entered or left except Mel's dad as he searched for work every day.

After four months in bed, Dr. Wade told Jerry and Amanda that he couldn't help. "If Mel is ever going to walk again, he has to get up and try." Mel's mom and dad got him out of bed, and with one on each side, dragged him around the house. Mentally anguished, Mel tried to move his feet, but they wouldn't respond. Finally, Mel managed a few steps. He began the painful process of relearning how to walk. Mel says, "This was a trying time for me. I was going to church, and I knew Jesus as my Savior, but since I'd never been discipled I didn't know how to go to Him for comfort and strength. But I felt like King David. The Lord knew him in the womb (Psalm 139), and He knew me too. God helped me despite not knowing how to draw close to Him during this difficult time.

In his sophomore and junior years, Mel attended Centennial High School and participated on the track team. He did well and lettered in the 220-yard dash and broad jump. God took Mel from being unable to walk to competing and winning in track! Meanwhile, Mel's dad found jobs trimming trees and doing yard work. People heated their homes burning either coal or wood which produced ash, and everyone had ash pits in the alleys behind their homes. Jerry cleaned the ash pits and used an old Studebaker to remove the waste to the city's dump. Mel helped his dad with trimming trees and cleaning out ash pits.

In 1933, President Franklin Roosevelt created the Works Progress Administration (WPA) to get people back to work. Jerry got a job as a night watchman on a building project along the Arkansas River in Pueblo. Concrete embankments were being built to control flooding from heavy rains. Today, those embankments still serve the city. Brother Jerry went to work for the Civilian Conservation Corps (CCC), another program that President Roosevelt created for young men ages seventeen to twenty-seven. Jerry quit school and moved to Wyoming to work as part of this program. The government paid for the workers' housing and food and gave them a salary in return for cutting down or replacing trees, grading roads and other jobs.[3] Jerry sent money home to his mom and dad to help the family out.

In 1942, tragedy struck. Mel's dad smoked heavily, using Bull Durham tobacco in hand-rolled cigarettes. Jerry developed pneumonia, and he would wake up at 5 a.m. coughing. One morning, in a violent coughing fit, he spit up half his lung. He went to the hospital but died at only forty-eight years old. Mel was sixteen and devastated. "I remember driving away from the cemetery in a big black hearse and looking back and seeing my dad's casket." Mel says, "I realized I would never see him again, and I wept and wept."

Jerry profoundly impacted his son's young life, instilling in him integrity, hard work, honesty, commitment, compassion, and unselfishness. Jerry's lack of education impacted him greatly during his lifetime, so he often talked with his children about completing their education. Mel remembers the last thing his dad told him, "Son, graduate from high school if you can. I don't know of anyone in the Sumrall family who has ever graduated from high school."

At the time, Mel could not know that God's amazing plans for him would include not only graduating from high school, but also completion of several degrees in higher education.

1. Dictionary of American History. The Gale Group, Inc. 2003. "Great Depression facts, information, pictures." Accessed April 12, 2017. https: www.encyclopedia.com/history/united-states-and-canada/us-history/great-depression.

2. 30 Dust Bowl Facts: U.S. History for Kids. http://www.american-historama.org/1929-1945-depression-ww2-era/dust-bowl.htm. Accessed April 12, 2017.

3. Youth work 1930's – The Economy and Youth. http://theyouthinthe1930s.weebly.com/youth-work-1930s.html. Accessed April 12, 2017.

Chapter 2

Mel the Marine – World War II

Following Jerry's death, Amanda got a job as a nurse's aide. Mel sacked groceries for Safeway after school. Mel's dad had told him about the attack on Pearl Harbor, and around town he heard rumors that the Japanese would invade the West Coast. Concerned about his mother and sisters, Mel quit school at the end of his junior year and joined the Marines in early 1943. His mother had to sign for him to join since he was only seventeen years old. Mel says, "I would have been drafted into the Army when I was eighteen years old, and I didn't want to be in some wimpy outfit. So I joined the Marines."

Mel boarded a bus for boot camp in San Diego. One of those infamous drill instructors met him and the other recruits at the station. The door opened, and the drill instructor stuck his head in and yelled, "Get out of there; line up!" So began this seventeen-year-old kid's military experience. His platoon, numbering seventy recruits, went through basic training together. "Corporal Cafarelli and PFC J. Taylor were my drill instructors," Mel says. "There's something about boot camp and the drill instructors that cause you to remember their names." The young men got in shape with lots of strenuous exercise including running. Mel had no problem running. In fact, he could run all day. Only four or five years earlier, he battled polio and could not walk at all.

After boot camp, Mel got a ten-day furlough to visit his mom. His brother Jerry was serving in the Navy at that time. His sister Myrtle had married, and Odetta had passed away. When his furlough ended, Mel was assigned to Marine Air Group 12 and sent to Guadalcanal. The officers told those in Marine Air Group 12 – 1st Marine Airwing that the Japanese were using Guadalcanal as a staging area to invade Australia and New Zealand. As he left the mainland on the aircraft carrier U.S.S. Barnes, Mel thought he would never see the shores of America again. As the ship neared the Equator, a Navy corpsman dropped a pill called Atebrin on the men's trays in the chow line. He told Mel, "Take it, now!" Mel learned later that the pill kept malaria from debilitating a person, but it did not prevent the disease altogether. Malaria usually struck the soldiers after they left the combat zone. "More Marines on Guadalcanal were probably lost to malaria than from bullets," Mel says.

Once Mel and his buddies arrived in Guadalcanal, they found the island mostly secured. They were sent to Esperitu Santos Island in the South Pacific where Mel's outfit received special training for the next three months. At this point in Mel's life, God was not in the picture very much. He does not remember sharing Christ with anyone, but he did tell people he was a Christian. Many Marines drank a lot and visited houses of ill repute, but Mel never did. During R&R Pepsi and beer were handed out, and Mel traded his beer for more Pepsi.

General Douglas MacArthur prepared to invade the Philippines, and he wanted to take a detachment of Marines with him. The detachment included Mel. As they deployed to accompany MacArthur, Mel saw American ships on the horizon off Hollandia, New Guinea, as far as he could see. Marine Air Group 12 landed with the invasion force at Leyte in the Philippines. From Leyte, Mel's unit moved on to Mindoro, an island off Luzon island. Then they went down to Zamboanga, a city in the far south of the country. Marine Air Group 12 participated in three major battles in the Philippines.

After eighteen months of combat, Mel was hit with shrapnel and also came down with malaria. He returned home on a hospital ship. As the ship neared port, the men rushed to the side to see America once again. Jubilation broke out on board. Once docked, Mel received a physical, a new uniform, and a thirty day furlough. During Mel's furlough, the first atom bomb was dropped on Hiroshima, then the second bomb was dropped on Nagasaki. Before the decision to bomb Hiroshima and Nagasaki, officials concluded that it would cost a million American lives to take Japan. Many people speculated that this dire prediction influenced President Truman's decision to use the bombs. Japan surrendered shortly after Nagasaki's destruction, as noted in the following statement:

On August 14, 1945, it was announced that Japan had surrendered unconditionally to the Allies, effectively ending World War II. Since then, both August 14 and August 15 have been known as "Victory over Japan Day," or simply "V-J Day." The term has also been used for September 2, 1945, when Japan's formal surrender took place aboard the U.S.S. Missouri, anchored in Tokyo Bay. Coming several months after the surrender of Nazi Germany, Japan's capitulation in the Pacific brought six years of hostilities to a final and highly anticipated close.[4]

Mel felt relieved when the war ended; he had had misgivings about going back to the South Pacific for another tour of duty. Having achieved the rank of corporal, Mel received an honorable discharged on November 28, 1945. He learned several life-lessons while serving in the Marines including the discipline to complete what he begins and to do his best. Branded on his heart is the Marine motto *Semper Fidelis*—Always Faithful. Loyalty to his country pumps through his veins. He doesn't merely believe in death before dishonor, but as a combat veteran he practiced it. Finally, the Marines equipped Mel with the leadership skills necessary for Mel to accomplish the good works God prepared for him to walk in.

After his discharge from the Marines, Mel wondered what he should do. His dad's last words rang in his ears, so he turned his attention to furthering his education.

---

1. V-J Day. Article. http://www.history.com/topics/world-war-ii/v-j-day. Accessed May 4, 2017.

Chapter 3

Education, Marriage, and Career

W hile World War II was still being fought, the Department of Labor estimated that, after the war, 15 million men and women who had been serving in the armed services would be unemployed. To reduce the possibility of postwar depression brought on by widespread unemployment, the National Resources Planning Board, a White House agency, studied postwar manpower needs as early as 1942 and in June 1943 recommended a series of programs for education and training. The American Legion designed the main features of what became the Serviceman's Readjustment Act and pushed it through Congress. Known as the G.I. Bill, the Serviceman's Readjustment Act provided stipends for tuition and books to returning veterans of World War II. The bill unanimously passed both chambers of Congress in the spring of 1944. President Franklin D. Roosevelt signed it into law on June 22, 1944, just days after the D-day invasion of Normandy.[5]

Mel took advantage of the G.I. Bill and started classes at Pueblo Junior College. Mel was able to enroll in college even though he hadn't finished high school; the colleges and universities wanted all the money they could get from the government. Mel finished a year and a half of college before he earned his high school degree. Uncertain what to study, Mel settled on engineering. The memory of that decision makes Mel chuckle. Mechanical engineering required algebra, analytical geometry, calculus, and trigonometry. Mel recalls, "I had trouble with math in high school. Even back in fourth grade I had trouble with long division."

One day, as Mel was resting on the grass, he saw a group of people waiting to register for classes. He noticed a beautiful young woman in the line (attractive women were called "slick chicks"). Most guys weren't so bold as to walk up to a girl and ask for a date, but this slick chick was in line with someone Mel knew: Shirley Ann Tappan. The next day, Mel asked Shirley Ann, "Who was that beautiful girl in line with you yesterday?"

"Oh, that's my cousin, Pittsburgh Pat."

"Would you be so kind as to introduce me to her?" Mel asked.

"Sure can," Shirley agreed

Shirley introduced Mel to Pittsburgh Pat. Their first date was less than romantic. Mel, president of the Engineers Club, invited Patty to a club meeting with him. She agreed and following the meeting they went to Melvin's Drive-In for something to eat. After dating for nine months, Mel proposed. Several months later, on August 25, 1946, they were married in Murraysville, Pennsylvania, a suburb of Pittsburgh. Mel and Patty visited Niagara Falls for a weeklong honeymoon. Mel drove a 1939 red Pontiac convertible. He had twenty-five dollars in his pocket. Gas cost nineteen cents a gallon, and the bed and breakfast where they stayed cost two dollars a night.

Mel eventually transferred to the University of Colorado in Boulder. Their first child, Susan, was born two years into their marriage. Although the G.I. Bill paid for Mel's books and tuition, the young couple only had seventy-five dollars a month for living expenses, not enough for a family of three to live on. Patty was majoring in chemistry, but she dropped out to work in a nursery for the next couple of years until Mel graduated in 1950. She would make many similar sacrifices in the years ahead.

After graduation, the family moved back to Pueblo where Mel landed a job as a metallurgist at Colorado Fuel & Iron Corporation (CF&I), one of the largest steel companies in the nation. The company had fourteen plants around the country. Mel joined a team tasked with investigating product failures in such things as the rails used by rail roads.

Meanwhile, the Korean War raged, and the Marines called Mel back to active duty shortly after he started at CF&I. The military sent Mel to an infantry base in Camp Pendleton, California. Since he had graduated from University of Colorado, one of his commanding officers, Captain Stover, wanted Mel in Korea as an officer. Mel explained that he had a wife and small daughter and asked if he could do something else. Captain Stover assigned Mel to train Marines at the base for combat in Korea. This lasted until the war ended in 1953.

Legally, companies had to rehire soldiers when they completed their military service. Mel returned to Colorado Fuel & Iron Corporation where he worked in a new thirty-million-dollar steel mill that produced oil well casings and tubing. Though Mel worked long hours at CF&I, he started building a house for his family patterned after a house he and Patty saw in San Diego. The house was on a corner and had two wings, each wing facing a different street. They bought land in the country in the Blende area of Pueblo, Colorado.

To save money, Mel built much of the house himself. In Colorado the foundation must sit below the freeze line—about thirty-one inches. Mel dug the foundation of the four thousand square foot house by hand with a shovel. He finished the garage first where the young family lived for the next several years. Susan was a toddler when Mel started the house, and Jerry came along while they were living in the garage. "There was no running water and no potty," Mel says. They had an outhouse, and Mel carried water in a five-gallon milk can from a neighbor's place. Patty washed dishes in a dishpan, then threw the dirty water in the front yard.

Once Mel completed the garage, he built an apartment for his widowed mother. It had a kitchen, living room, and bedroom. His mom moved in and lived there for quite a while until she took a job in Colorado Springs. Mel and Patty moved into the apartment while Mel continued to build the rest of the house. Mel designed the house with some modern features including a glass block wall in the living room. Eventually, the house had two fireplaces, five bedrooms, a big kitchen, a large living room, and a dining room

Since city water wasn't available, Mel dug his own well. He poured circular concrete forms three feet tall. Each form had holes so the water could come in through the bottom. Mel put the first circular form down and got inside of it to scoop out gravel, put it in a bucket, and dump it outside the well. Eventually, the hole became too deep for him to dump the waste. Mel used a pulley to get the bucket of gravel to the top where Patty, who was pregnant, stood nearby and dumped the buckets. Mel worked long hours at the steel mill, then came home to dig the well. After many months, he finally hit water at twenty-two feet.

"Once we got water, we could do all kinds of things," Mel says.

Next, Mel considered how best to heat the house. "I didn't want to have forced air heat, because the humidity is so low in the wintertime. In the morning your nose and throat are dried out. I decided to put in a hot water circulating system. I put a unit out in the garage that would pump hot water throughout the system that I ran all along the exterior of the house. I had a special thermostat for Mama's apartment, and I had a thermostat for the garage that we could turn to whatever temperature we wished." Mel wanted to dress up the cinder-block backside of the house. He hauled moss rocks from the mountains and laid them against the house. During the summer, he kept them wet, allowing the moss to grow. He also designed a waterfall that circulated the water.

Going through the poverty of the Depression impacted Mel. He felt dissatisfied with each new job position and strived to keep moving up in his company. Mel supervised hundreds of employees and had personal relationships with many of his workers as well as their families. He had a piercing operator named Felipe Ramirez who ran a piece of equipment called a piercing mill. This machine pushed a hot billet about six feet long between rolls to make a hole in the billet from end to end. One day, Felipe showed up drunk. He mishandled his machine and almost killed a man. Felipe's wife used to call Mel and ask if her husband had received his check that day. Then, she'd say, "Well, I guess he's at the tavern drinking it up; we won't have any food to eat this week."

After the accident, Mel had to fire Felipe, but Mel said to him, "Felipe, I care about you, and I want to help you. You go to the state hospital and get cured of your alcohol problem. Come back in a month or two months or whatever it is, and I'll give your job back to you." Felipe did, and Mel rehired him. Later, Felipe became the chairman of Alcoholics Anonymous for Southern Colorado. Mel saw the value of each person and recognized the investment of the company in its employees. Mel only fired two people in his twenty-five years with CF&I, and he rehired both.

Good money could be made in production management, so Mel transferred. He progressed from general foreman, to assistant superintendent, and then superintendent. Mel learned to work with people from different nationalities including Italian, Polish, Czech, Hispanic, and many other backgrounds. Each culture required unique handling to ensure the best productivity. Mel also learned the importance of good communication. This training ground in leadership and diverse populations would prove useful to Mel later in ministry.

Regarding CF&I Mel says, "It was a challenge, but I enjoyed it. However, it was very difficult at times because the union was very strong." Toward the end of Mel's career at CF&I, striking unions across the country hurt America. "It was the beginning of the downfall of unions in America," Mel says. "The steel industry in America was being challenged by steel companies in other countries." When contracts ended, the unions said, "Give us what we want, or we'll strike." Management told them to go ahead. The strikes lasted months. Finally, President Nixon called the union heads and management to the White House. He locked them in a room with Marines at the door until they settled. The unions got almost everything they wanted. As a result, the steel industry died in America. It could no longer compete with cheaper foreign steel. Companies couldn't make money, and plants shut down, affecting the entire country.

As Mel continued to get promotions at CF&I, he had no idea that a huge change was coming to the Sumrall family, one that would take Mel and Patty on the adventure of a lifetime.

---

1. Serviceman's Readjustment Act (1944). https://www.ourdocuments.gov/doc.php?flash=true&doc=76. Accessed May 6, 2017.

Chapter 4

Heartache, Spiritual Growth and a New Direction

U sually Mel worked on Sunday mornings. Patty took Susan and Jerry, the two children they had at the time, to church. One Sunday Patty came home and told Mel, "Honey, the pastor said this morning that we could have a personal relationship with Jesus."

"Yeah, that's right. I'm a Christian," Mel said.

"I didn't know that. Would it be all right for me to do that?" Patty asked.

"Of course," Mel said.

Mel tried to live a godly life, but he never acknowledged Christ, talked about Him, or served Him. The lack of discipleship in Mel's life stunted his spiritual growth so much that his own wife didn't know she could have a personal relationship with Jesus. When Mel made his profession of faith thirty years earlier, no one talked to him about sharing his faith.

Fifteen years passed as Mel continued working in the steel mill. During this time, their family grew to include three more children: Karen, Laura, and Pamela. Mel spent long hours at CF&I, but he and Patty still took the kids camping and skiing occasionally. "There weren't the variety of campers on the market like there is today," Mel recalls. "We had an Airstream called the Silver Bullet. Patty and I would pile all the kids in it, and we'd go out and park along the trout streams in Colorado and go fly fishing and do S'mores around the campfire. We would tie a rope around the kids, one after another, and then tie them to a bush so they wouldn't fall in the river. The things we started with our kids, they're continuing to do. And they have always wanted us to be part of it. It keeps the family together. Remember that verse, 'Train up a child when he's young, and when he's old he won't depart from it.'" (Proverbs 22:6)

Their last child, Pamela, was born when Mel and Patty were 38 years old. Pamela suddenly became ill when she was nine months old. Patty took her to the doctor that fateful morning. Mel said, "We watched her die that afternoon." The doctor who delivered Pamela told Mel and Patty that learning the cause of Pamela's death might help other children. They made the difficult decision to allow an autopsy on little Pamela. They learned that she had died of a heart attack caused by a viral infection called Coxsackie which attacked her heart. After the autopsy, Mel and Patty buried their baby.

A deep depression settled over Mel. He lived with guilt and remorse, thinking Pamela would have lived had they gotten her to the hospital sooner. Mel's spiritual immaturity hindered him from finding comfort by drawing close to the Lord. Mel wrote the following inscription in 1963 in the devotional *Streams in the Desert*:

"My precious child Pamela has died. I am in a deep depression and don't know which way to turn. Oh, God, I am your child, please hear my cry. I confess that I am unworthy of your kindness and faithfulness, but Lord, I have no one else to turn to. Please comfort and give me hope and direction for the future" (Ps 78:72), (2 Chron 14:11). God would eventually answer his prayer, but not as he expected.

At this time, Mel's company insisted that all upper management participate in some type of community service. Mel wanted to help School District 70 in Pueblo get some new buildings built. The district held two bond elections, but both failed. Mel decided to run for the school board and won. The Lord was stretching Mel and teaching him the skills needed for future ministry. He eventually became president of the school board where he served for six years. (He still has the gavel he used as president.) Mel wanted to better understand the hiring process. He attended the interviews for a teaching position in District 70 and met an applicant, Ron Chadwick.

Ron had his Bible with him, and immediately he and Mel felt drawn together. Mel told him about Pamela dying, and Ron came alongside Mel to disciple him.

Mel commented, "If it had not been for Ron Chadwick, I don't know what would have happened to me. He was with me for only eighteen months, but in that time, God used him to totally turn my life around." Mel and Patty frequently got together with Ron and his wife Sally for dinner and fellowship. During the depths of Mel's depression, he often called Ron Chadwick. "Sometimes when I called Ron," Mel says, "I'd be crying." When Ron got those distressing calls he'd say, "Where are you, Mel?" Ron would meet with Mel and comfort him by reading from Psalms or somewhere else in Scripture. Ron's loving care during those difficult times so changed Mel that he told the Lord, "If I ever have anything to do with leadership in a church, we will major on discipleship."

Mel watched his 80-year-old pastor do everything at the church by himself. He did all the marrying, burying, preaching, teaching, and on and on. Mel asked Ron, "Why doesn't God give Pastor Edwards anyone to help him?" Ron turned to Ephesians 4:11-12 and read, "And He gave some as apostles, and some as prophets, and some as evangelists, and some as pastors and teachers, for the equipping of the saints for the work of service, to the building up of the body of Christ." The light came on for Mel and he exclaimed, "Well, Ron, we're doing church all wrong in America. I don't know of anybody that has that kind of emphasis in their congregation." Two convictions took root in Mel's heart: The importance of discipleship and the necessity to equip the saints to do the work of the ministry. Those two convictions would later impact Denton Bible Church in a huge way.

After eighteen months, Ron resigned from his job with District 70. As Ron prepared to leave for his new position at Calvary Bible College in Missouri, he handed Mel his Sunday school materials and said, "You're the new teacher."

Mel responded, "Ron, I don't know anything about teaching the Bible."

Ron replied, "That's all right. You'll learn to teach it. The Lord will help you. If you need anything, get in touch with me." Ron added a cryptic comment, "I don't believe you belong in the business world. I think you belong in the pastorate."

Ron planted this seed of an idea and it grew in Mel's heart. One day, Mel came home from work and told Patty, "Sweetheart, I think God might be calling us to go into full-time ministry. What would you think of that?"

She smiled, "Oh, I've already told the Lord I'd go anyplace He wants to take you."

Mel comments, "So many wives would have thought about other things, but Patty was willing to give up her friends, the church we were in at the time, living in Colorado, and financial security which meant she would have to go to work. She said to me, 'What would it entail?' I told her, 'Probably going to seminary where you will look at the back of my head for four years while I study.' Patty asked me where, and I told her Dallas. Patty replied, 'Oh, that would be much better. I thought it would probably be a grass hut somewhere out in New Guinea.'" Mel appreciated Patty's flexibility. She rolled with the punches.

Before his departure, Ron mentioned that Howard Hendricks and his wife Jeanne were visiting Navigators headquarters in Colorado Springs. Ron asked Mel if he would like to meet them. Mel had heard so much about this Dallas Theological Seminary (DTS) professor that he couldn't wait to meet him. They had dinner with Prof (as he was affectionately known at DTS) and Jeanne, and Mel told Prof that he felt the Lord tugging him to seminary. Prof got excited. In those days, men stayed with the same company forty or fifty years and then retired. Folks didn't have a second or third career like they do today.

During dessert, Prof said, "Mel, let me tell you something, son. I'd love to have you come to seminary. That would really be great. But you shouldn't come to seminary because you think Howard Hendricks wants you to come to seminary."

Mel's antenna went up at that, and he asked Prof, "Why is that?"

Prof told him, "Because the going will get rough, and when it gets rough if you know the Lord wants you there, you can stick it out. But if not, you'll probably fold and go do something else."

Through the years, Mel has shared this advice with hundreds of men interested in ministry.

Mel suddenly remembered a promise he'd made the Lord years earlier while aboard a ship in the South Pacific during World War II. Facing the possibility of death, he told the Lord, "If I make it through this war, I'll serve You the rest of my life." After the war ended, Mel forgot his promise.

Mel realized God had used the tragic death of little Pamela to get his attention. He knew the Lord was calling him into the ministry. He had to go.

Chapter 5

From Seminary Student to Pastor

Mel became an elder in the little church he and Patty attended. Mel says, "I was well-educated, probably the only elder who had a university degree. I was trying to be as faithful to the Lord in every area as I could. In the life of an elder, what would that look like? One of the things I did was to hug people in order to try to set an atmosphere." Mel chose to become "a hugger." Some men felt uneasy receiving hugs, but no one offered negative feedback. Today Mel still gives bear hugs to men and women alike. Many people respond, "I needed that!"

Ron challenged Mel to apply to Dallas Theological Seminary. At forty years old, Mel received an acceptance letter; however, he declined the offer. Though Mel knew the Lord was calling him to DTS, he hesitated because of the foreign language requirements. Without a Bible college background, he felt apprehensive studying Greek and Hebrew. Mel says, "That showed my lack of faith at the time. I should have realized that if God was calling me to DTS, He would give me what it took to get through the languages."

His concerns regarding three years of Greek and two years of Hebrew and all that theology drove Mel to prayer. It's just as if the Lord said, "Is there an Orthodox synagogue in this town?"

"Yes, Lord."

"Well, why don't you go talk to a rabbi there and see if he'll teach you some Hebrew."

Mel talked to Rabbi Nathaniel Pollack and told him, "I'm a Christian, and I want to serve Christ. I want to go to seminary, but I need some help with Hebrew before I go. Would you be willing to help me?"

"Oh, I'd be delighted to," Rabbi Pollack said.

He taught Mel two years of Hebrew, but Mel still faced the challenge of Greek. So, he prayed again. "Is there a Greek Orthodox church in your town?" the Lord asked.

Mel found Father Churis at a Greek Orthodox Church. Father Churis came from Athens, Greece. Mel asked him, "Father Churis, would you teach me some Greek? I want to go to seminary, and I want to get a head start."

Father Churis replied, "Oh, you betcha!"

Mel spent two years studying Greek with him. Neither Rabbi Pollack nor Father Churis charged Mel for language lessons. Mel says, "It was amazing. Here I was having all these doubts, and God had already prepared a way. I didn't need to have those doubts. When I got to seminary, I began the foreign languages with a head start. Those foreign languages will eat your lunch as far as being time consuming. You must learn, in Greek for example, a chart about two feet by three feet, of all kinds of tenses and moods, and that's how you determine what the Greek really says. In Greek they don't start off with a subject, verb and direct object like we do. They start off with what they want to emphasize. Some of the verses start off, 'God,' and that's who they're going to talk about. And that's how it comes out in the Greek. It was a big help for me when I started seminary to have had some training in the languages."

A few years later, Mel decided to reapply to DTS. He received an acceptance letter, but he also received a letter from Ron Chadwick asking for financial help in getting his Ph.D. "I was so thankful to Ron," Mel said, "that I decided we would help him. I wrote the seminary and told them I couldn't come at this time." Bob Dean, the pastor of Mel and Patty's church, had a son who wanted to go to Bible college, but Bob couldn't afford to send him. Mel continued to postpone his own education at seminary to help Bob's boy.

Eight years after his first acceptance at DTS, Mel applied for the third time and was admitted. He and Patty moved to Dallas, and Mel enrolled as the oldest student at forty-eight years of age. Mel says, "After I got to the seminary and got close to some of the professors, Dr. Williams was talking to me and said, 'You know, Mel, you shouldn't have been accepted because of your age.'"

Mel credits his education at Dallas Theological Seminary with giving him the foundation for his lengthy years of ministry. Many professors at DTS greatly impacted Mel. Dr. Ed Diebler taught church history, and Mel recalls how much Dr. Diebler loved his students. "We'd sing a hymn before we started class. He and I were close; we often went fishing together." Dr. Haddon Robinson, author of *Biblical Preaching*, taught Expository Preaching at DTS. He developed an approach to Scripture known as "the big idea." He instructed students to go paragraph by paragraph, talking about the same idea using short sentences. Students emphasized the big idea several times throughout the message, especially in the conclusion. According to Mel, Tommy follows this model of preaching. Dr. John Walvoord was serving as president of DTS, and he touched Mel's life. "Dr. Walvoord was the guiding light, the one who led the men at DTS and set an example for them," Mel says.

Dr. Bruce Waltke, who taught both Hebrew and church history, was so brilliant that he had a difficult time instructing on the students' level. "The course covered Documentary Hypothesis which had to do with things like Moses not really writing the first five books of the Bible," Mel said. "Dr. Waltke made up the mid-term exam. It was so difficult that I didn't understand the questions. I wrote at the top of my paper, 'Prof, I did the best I could. I'm not sure I even understand what you're asking.'" Mel continues, "The questions weren't something we covered in class. Dr. Waltke expected the students to apply principles to a certain situation that he'd taught using a totally different situation." The final came, but the men still didn't have grades from the mid-term exam. Dr. Waltke provided the material for the final, but on the day of the test, Dr. Waltke said, "Men, I thought it would be an insult to give you the final I made up for you, so I changed it. The first one was too easy." Mel passed the course, but many students didn't.

Two professors, Dr. Dwight Pentecost and Dr. Philip Williams also pastored churches. "This helped me a lot," Mel says. "If you're a pastor, you have a pastor's heart, and your teaching comes from making application from the Scriptures." Another positive influence at DTS was Dr. Elliott Johnson who taught Bible Exposition. Mel says, "It was always a joy to go to his class. His exposition of Scripture was clear and convincing. He had the ability to make you want to learn; it was never boring. All the students loved him because of his warm manner."

Dr. Scott Horrell, a longtime DTS professor, was a classmate of Mel's. He remembers, "Mel was well known for having left a fairly lucrative position in the industrial world to come to Dallas Theological Seminary, so he had the age edge on most of the rest of us. He was a natural leader with maturity and a big vision for the work of our Lord. Even more so, it was his love for fellow students and his warmth in our Savior that endeared us to him. I was much involved in world missions in those days and perhaps that drew us together. But Mel had a shepherd's heart then, and that has continued to this day. What I probably didn't see, because we were in classes at seminary, was his evangelistic passion." In 2017, Mel and Dr. Horrell celebrated the fortieth anniversary of their graduation from DTS. "It was a privilege to stand together and rejoice in what God has done," Dr. Horrell says. "Denton Bible Church pulsates even yet with Mel's passion to reach the world for Christ."

Mel wondered how well he'd be received by his classmates since he was old enough to be their father. However, they loved Mel and elected him as president of the class his first and second year at DTS. The third year Mel was elected vice president of the student body. He could have been president of the student body his fourth year, but God had other plans.

When Mel arrived at DTS, the academic dean, Dr. Campbell, said, "Mel, we want to send you out to preach on weekends."

Mel told him, "Now wait a minute. If I knew how to do that, I probably wouldn't be here. You've got to give me a couple of years before you send me out."

Dr. Campbell agreed, but he didn't forget. Two years later, Dr. Campbell said, "Mel, you've had two years training. There's a group of four or five guys coming to the seminary from Denton, and they're looking for a pastor for their church. They want the oldest man we've got, and you're it. How about meeting with these guys?" When Mel met them, he learned they had a Methodist background. He told them, "Now you realize that my doctrine is not going to be like your doctrine because I'm going to stay real close to the Bible." They replied, "Oh, that's all right. We don't know anything about the Bible anyway." Sadly, they were right.

On weekends Mel and Patty drove to Bell Avenue Memorial Church and taught the congregation. If a crisis occurred, such as a death, he would come during the week as well. The congregation numbered about twenty-five people when Mel started as pastor. A year later, it had grown to a hundred and fifty people, mostly university students. Mel performed his first wedding at Bell Avenue Memorial Church. Unfortunately, somebody spilled soda pop on the carpet and the older people got upset. They informed Mel there would be no more weddings in the church.

Mel told Dr. Campbell what happened. Mel said, "I'm not going to put up with this." Dr. Campbell replied, "Well, OK, just start a new church in Denton." Unknowingly, Dr. Campbell's exhortation would eventually affect thousands of people. Mel did as Dr. Campbell suggested, and Denton Bible Church was born in 1976 during Mel's last year in seminary.

"I just had to start a church," Mel says. "This was in the 1970's when there weren't many churches doing discipleship and equipping the saints." Mel remembered his promise to the Lord that if he ever became a pastor, he would major on discipleship and equipping the saints for the work of the ministry. "Starting a church from scratch is one of the most difficult ministries you can imagine," Mel says. "You don't have enough people to have a salary to support your family. You must find a place to meet. It was a very difficult time."

Mel could have chosen an easier situation. A church east of Dallas asked Dr. Deibler, Mel's professor, to come pastor them. He said to Mel, "Why don't you come with me and help out for a couple of years?" Mel declined. Plenty of people would eagerly join Dr. Diebler in a beautiful new church building close to Lake Ray Hubbard, but no one from DTS was headed to Denton where the going would be rough. Mel chose Denton.

Years earlier, God had prepared a way for Mel and Patty to have an income until Denton Bible Church grew enough to support them. When Patty withdrew from college, Mel promised she could finish her education once the kids started grade school. Patty had majored in chemistry before dropping out. When the time came for Patty to resume her education, Mel said, "Honey, you're going back to college to get your Master's. What if something should happen to me, and I died young. How would you support yourself and the children?" At that time, jobs utilizing a degree in chemistry required relocating to a city like Houston with a strong petroleum industry. Mel asked Patty, "Don't you think you ought to reconsider your major?"

Patty said, "Yes, Honey, I think you're right." Patty changed her major to Childhood Education which was beneficial and providential. Patty taught school at Trinity Christian Academy in north Dallas to help support the family during the first nine years of Denton Bible Church, from 1976 to 1985.

In May 1976, a couple of dozen people from Bell Avenue Memorial Church attended the launch of Denton Bible Church. One of the original couples, Scott and Sharon Dumas remembers, "Al and Chris Baker and another couple plus a single guy from DTS were helping Mel at Bell Avenue by teaching Sunday school. Members of Bell Avenue who came with us were Jay and Harriett Armstrong and Chuck and Jennifer Couch in addition to Jim Ligierri (married to Beth), who was single at the time. John and Carolyn Prather and David and Jill Perez were two of the couples plus a group of singles." They met at Oak Street Hall on the North Texas campus where Scott worked. The attendees settled on *Denton Bible Church* as the official name and established the doctrinal statement. For two or three weeks, the church met on the campus, then moved to the Firehouse Theatre where Jim Ligierri had an office as an inspector for the city.

Denton Bible Church has never taken up an offering. In the beginning Styrofoam ice chests were placed at the back of the building for people to deposit their offering. Today DBC has wooden offering boxes at each door of the sanctuary, however, Styrofoam ice chests are still used for special collections (called Heave-Ho Sunday) to fund buildings. Historically, members have given generously, allowing DBC to pay off every building that has been built.

Dr. Gene Getz, one of Mel's professors at DTS, developed the concept of "one anothers" which significantly impacted Mel. Dr. Getz explains, "When I was at Dallas Seminary in the late 1960's, early 1970's, I was challenged by the students in terms of the relevancy of the church. That's when I wrote *Sharpening the Focus of the Church*. That led me to start Fellowship Bible Church which I never planned to start." Dr. Getz continues, "After being a professor for twenty years (thirteen years at Moody and seven years at Dallas Seminary), I became a full-time, church-planting pastor. In the process of researching the church, I came across the word *allanon* in the New Testament which is translated "one another." I found that it appears sixty times. I began to read that in terms of the body of Christ. Paul used the word about forty times as to what we're to do for one another."

Dr. Getz included a list of the "one anothers" in *Sharpening the Focus of the Church*. As he began church planting, he taught a series of messages based upon the "one anothers." The messages eventually became books which are *Building Up One Another*, *Praying for One Another*, *Encouraging One Another*, *Serving One Another*, and *Loving One Another*. Mel continues to talk about and teach the concept of the "one anothers" today. He says, "The 'one anothers' is the code of conduct for Christians as we interact with the body of Christ to bring unity. I'm grateful to Dr. Getz for passing on this vital concept in my training at Dallas Seminary." These simple foundations would shape Denton Bible's future in the decades to come.

More university students began attending as Denton Bible continued to grow. Soon, the Lord would provide someone on staff who could minister to them and be a trusted, lifelong friend and partner for Mel. Denton Bible Church would never be the same.

Chapter 6

Tommy Enters the Scene as God Grows DBC

After meeting at the Firehouse Theatre for a few weeks, Denton Bible Church moved to the Methodist Student Center at North Texas. Various congregations, including a Jewish synagogue and a Methodist church, met there for the summer since most students headed home. As summer progressed, Denton Bible Church grew to around eighty people. In late August, classes resumed, and students from the other ministries began attending DBC. Officials from those ministries came to Mel and said, "You're taking all our people." They insisted DBC move. The church settled in the Optimist Gym and stayed there from late 1976 to 1978.

DBC had existed for a year and a half when Mel was introduced to Tommy Nelson. Around a hundred people, mostly college-aged, attended DBC at this point. Denton provides a home to both the University of North Texas (UNT) and Texas Woman's University (TWU). These universities had ministries on campus such as Campus Crusade for Christ, Navigators, and Intervarsity. Most of the university students coming to DBC had contact with one of these para-church organizations.

Mel recalls, "One day a number of older people came to church. After the service I asked them, 'Where do you folks come from?'" They told Mel they went to a Methodist church, but it split. The Methodist headquarters assigned a new pastor without any input from the congregation. The new guy didn't believe in the deity of Christ, among other things. They told Mel they couldn't stay under that teaching, so they left. As Mel talked to them, they told him about a young man, Tommy Nelson, teaching college students at the Methodist church. God put someone in Tommy's life who told him about Mel and Denton Bible Church. Either Mel got in touch with Tommy or vice versa. Either way, they met at Denny's on I-35.

Mel says, "The Lord put us together so well that after I met with Tommy, I went and talked to the four elders we had at the time: Tim Jenkins, Steve Cheek, Jim Boso and Chuck Couch. I told them, 'I found someone that could teach the college students.' Then I told them about Tommy's background as a quarterback at UNT. One of the elders said, 'Do we really want a jock for a pastor?' Thankfully, they hired Tommy despite his being a jock!"

Tommy was in his first semester at Dallas Seminary and was sleeping on the floor at Greg Talkington's home, an early member of DBC. Tommy and his wife, Teresa, had one son, Ben, at the time. When Tommy started seminary, Teresa and Ben moved in with her parents in East Texas. After Tommy joined the DBC staff, Teresa and Ben returned to Denton, and the Nelsons rented a house next door to Mel and Patty on Selene street.

Mel and Tommy grew together during that time; both emphasized prayer. They never prayed for a big church; instead, they wanted to reach the community and the world for Christ. Denton Bible Church continued to grow in the rented space at Optimist Gym on Highway 377. The church body numbered around a hundred and fifty people, including some older couples with children. The facility had only one room for Sunday school—a small room about the size of a living room. Other groups rented the Optimist Gym during the week, including a motorcycle gang on Saturdays. DBC members had to sweep up the beer cans, pop bottles and other trash on Sunday mornings, not a very inviting place for children's ministry.

"The smell of alcohol would knock you down when you came in the door," Mel remembers. A karate club met there, too, and they'd pull the paper towel holders off the wall and knock the doors down. Mel laughs, "It was like the Wild West days!" One day after service, a mom and dad with tears rolling down their cheeks told Mel, "We have to leave DBC because there's no place for our children to be ministered to." Right then, Mel learned parents will endure almost anything if the children are well taken care of. Mel and Tommy realized they needed more room for the kids. They rented space at Camp Copas, about eight miles outside of Denton. However, the move caused DBC to lose college students; the commute was too difficult for many of them.

Jim Boso, who was the manager of KDNT radio station in Denton, called Mel one day and said, "Hey, Mel, there's some ground up for sale on University Drive. Somebody died, and the land is in a will. There's about three and a half acres. I think we ought to get that three and a half acres."

Mel says, "I'm sure the rest of us laughed. We had a large congregation of college kids, the poorest people in the world. The land cost $43,500 (a huge amount back then)."

But they prayed and said, "We'll see what God will do." Mel recalls getting the congregation together, marching around the property, and claiming it for the Lord like Joshua and the Israelites did Jericho. College kids in the congregation sold their musical instruments. Several couples sold their portable sound systems and gave the money to help buy the land. A couple of college girls called their parents and said, "My church needs some money to buy some ground to build our church on." Parents sent money. Teresa's dad owned an oil company, and her parents gave DBC $15,000 toward the land. The down payment of $22,000 was raised. Mel still has a soft spot in his heart for college students because of the sacrifices those students made.

Mel and Tommy didn't know where the second half would come from, but they started clearing the land. Foliage and trees flourished everywhere. Jack George, Sr., a member of the congregation, helped clear the land with his tractor. He had cancer and a catheter hung down his leg, but he was there—riding his tractor. Mel recalls the wonderful time of closeness and fellowship DBC experienced during this phase. He comments, "On Saturdays the guys would hack and rake and tow stuff out of there, and you'd get stickers and brambles all over you, and branches would be hitting your face. At noontime, the sisters would have lunch for us, and we'd have a time of fellowship. It was a sweet time."

The balance of the loan came due, and God provided the money to pay off the land. Mel got a call from the vice president at Citizens National Bank in Denton. He said, "I'm vice president of Citizens National Bank, and I noticed you bought some land on University. I think churches are good for the community, and I'd like to loan you the money to build your first building. I'm going to let you have it at the Federal Reserve discount rate, which is what the banks get." Naturally, everyone felt elated.

The steel work, electrical, and plumbing required contractors, but members of the congregation came together for most of the work on the building. Nolan Barnett, a DBC member, knew construction, and he served as superintendent, getting permits and overseeing the work. The congregation did all the framing, hanging drywall, and whatever they could handle. Mel recalls that some of the guys—and he thinks Tommy was one of them—didn't know which end of a hammer to use. Construction did not always go smoothly. John Bordeaux stepped through the ceiling as he helped Mel put in the air conditioner. The church met in the new building as soon as it was closed in. The facility had no heat yet, so people would bring blankets and cover up. Mel says, "There was light from bare bulbs hanging from the ceiling. It was like camping out, but we were having a wonderful time."

Ray and Nellyne McFarlane found Denton Bible Church in October 1981. "There were about one hundred-fifty people at that time, probably ninety-eight percent college kids," Ray says. They remember the unfinished building, helping hang sheetrock, and working on flower beds. Three months later, Mel invited the McFarlanes to his home for a Bible study. "That's what we were wanting," Ray says. "We went to Mel's and discovered it was a *Colossians 2:7* study, the discipleship course that DBC uses. We joined four other couples, and Mel handed the group off to Bob Wilson, so we met at his house the next week."

Nellyne worked with Teresa Nelson teaching Sunday school to fourth, fifth and sixth graders. In 1983 Mel asked Ray to be a deacon over facilities. In 1985, Ray was asked to serve as an elder, which he did until 1999. "Mel had his finger on the pulse of the church," Nellyne comments. She remembers Mel telling her and Ray exactly what they needed. "That made a big impact on us," she says. "Here's a man that loved us so much that he would address the things that needed to be changed in our lives." Ray and Nellyne learned perseverance from Mel. "He has never given up," says Ray. "When he retired from staff he sure didn't quit working. He taught over and over that the word retirement is not in the Bible. I look up to Mel as a father figure. He has a pastor's heart, full of love and compassion. Tommy does also, but in a different way."

The first building, known as the Sumrall Center today, was officially launched on Easter Sunday 1982. Many expansions of Denton Bible Church would follow as the Lord continued to grow the congregation. Once the church had a permanent home, Mel considered how he could further fulfill his promise to the Lord to disciple the saints and equip them to do the work of the ministry.

Chapter 7

The Beginning of Discipleship and Equipping the Saints

As God grew Denton Bible Church, Mel focused on the Great Commission through making disciples. When Mel and Patty moved into their new home on Bonnie Brae in 1978, they discipled young women by having them live with them. Over a thirty-five-year period, seventy-eight young women stayed with Mel and Patty in their two upstairs bedrooms. The first woman to do so was Jean Terrell (formerly McKee) who lived with Mel and Patty from June 1979 through May 1980. Jean remembers, "A friend invited me to Denton Bible Church in the spring of 1978. Mel preached, and the church met in the Optimist Gym. I'd been in church all my life, but I'd never heard a sermon like that. I never went anywhere else."

As their surrogate dad, Mel requested he be allowed to interview guys who wanted to go out with them. In January 1980, Jean met Kevan Bower in a *Life of Jesus* class at the Baptist Student Union at UNT. He wanted to go out with her, but she told him he had to meet Mel first. "Kevan came over and Mel took him out in the garage while I sat in the living room," Jean recalls. "I was sweating blood while I waited. Eventually Mel came inside and said, 'His dad is a DTS guy. It's all good.'"

Together, Mel and Tommy performed Jean and Kevan's wedding two years later. Sadly, Kevan died of brain cancer three years and three months after their wedding. They were living near Kevan's family

52

in Houston where Kevan received treatment at the VA Hospital. Mel came to Houston to do the funeral. After Kevan passed away, Jean moved back to Denton and lived with Kay and Chris Littler and their daughter until she got back on her feet. Eventually, Jean started dating Paul Terrell, Kevan's roommate at one time. They married, with Mel and Tommy once again performing the wedding. Paul and Jean just celebrated their thirtieth anniversary.

Another young woman who lived with Mel and Patty was Ann Bateman. She was a missionary kid who grew up in Taiwan and moved to Denton to attend UNT. Ann says, "I lived with Mel and Patty for two years. They were like the best grandparents you could have. Mel is like a compassionate grandpa." Ann dated Dan Toepperwein, a student at UNT and a DBC attendee. He often came to Mel and Patty's home. Dan would call Tommy with a question, and if Tommy didn't know the answer, he'd raise the window and yell, "Hey, Mel, I have a question for you."

Dan tells the story of a friend of his who had a 4.0 average. "She knew I went to DBC and asked me, 'Aren't you going to invite me to church?' DBC met at Camp Copus in an old-fashioned white clapboard building. Mel got up to preach. He used an overhead projector and a Marks-A-Lot to draw the hand of God dangling a stick figure over hell as he explained the gospel. I was hoping Mel would hit it out of the park with some deep theological sermon that would reach my intellectual friend. I squirmed as Mel drew the stick figure." Dan's friend trusted Christ as her Savior that Sunday.

Dan compares Mel to the Apostle Paul. "Mel had a Damascus road experience that led him into the ministry. He can go into a room, walk up and down, shake hands, and meet people like I imagine Paul did. God uses Mel to bring people to Christ and plant churches wherever he goes, even when he's fly fishing in Colorado." Ann remembers, "The college kids spent hours and hours talking theology. Tommy was at seminary; he would go to class and then teach them what he had learned."

Dan and Ann were married in 1982 in Taiwan by her father. Mel inspired Dan to go to Dallas Theological Seminary and become a pastor. Gratitude fills their hearts for Mel, Patty, Tommy, and Teresa for pouring into them in their younger years. Over a four-year period,

Tommy and Teresa discipled young men who lived with them, reasoning that because of his young age, it would not be appropriate to have young women living with them.

Mel and Tommy prayed about finding discipleship materials for the folks at Denton Bible Church—especially for husbands and wives. There was not an overabundance of discipleship materials on the market then like there is now. God answered their prayer in a magnificent way.

Mel and Patty headed to Colorado, their favorite spot for some much-needed R & R. They stayed at the beautiful grounds of Glen Eyrie, the Navigator headquarters, planning on kicking back and getting some rest. Their first day at the Glen, Mel and Patty attended an orientation meeting with fifty people to receive their schedule for the week. Their days would include breakfast, quiet time, and chapel service followed by small group discussions of the message. The afternoon allowed free time—unless a person was qualified and wanted training to start a ministry at their church called *Colossians 2:7*. The material could only be used after completing the training. While other people fished and hiked, Mel sat through the *2:7* course, taught by Mel Leader, a staffer with the Navigators. Even though he'd gone to seminary, he still had to attend the sessions. In the evenings, Mel prepared for the next day's program. Though it wasn't a very restful week, he went through two books of 2:7, leaving Glen Eyrie qualified to teach 2:7 at DBC. The first edition of *2:7* had five books and participants memorized sixty-seven verses; the current version consists of three books and seventeen memory verses.

Seven couples signed up for the first *2:7* group at DBC. They were Jack and Vonnie George, Todd and Louise Judy, Jim and Fairlyon Hill, Ron and Teri Patton, Buster and Lou Garrett, Pete and Angie Peters, and Jim and Marie Hoffpauer. What should have taken two years stretched into four years. Laughing, someone asked Mel, "You know why we get off on all these rabbit trails?"

Mel responded, "Well, I thought it was because you wanted to know something."

"No, we didn't want to break up the group."

The seven couples and the Sumralls became close friends as they grew spiritually through *2:7*. After the group graduated in 1986,

Mel and Patty planned to take them to Israel. Because of tensions in the Middle East, instead they took them to Purgatory Ski Resort in Colorado. They joked, "Instead of Mel and Patty taking us to the Holy Land, they took us to Purgatory," Of course, Mel and Patty were veteran skiers, along with the Pattons and the Peters. The rest of the group took skiing lessons.

Vonnie George remembers the trip. "We trained on the lower slopes, and then our instructor said, 'Everyone can go to the top of the hill except Buster.' Well, there was no way that Buster, who was bigger than the rest of us, was going to stay on the bottom of the hill when everyone else was going to the top. He was a big old guy who worked as a welder on the Alaska pipeline." Mel told them, "You have to know how to get on and off the lift, or you'll fall every time. And you must know how to make turns and how to stop when you're skiing. "Buster evidently had not mastered all of that," Vonnie recalls. "Mel and Patty were watching us ski down the upper slope. We were making the turns, and it was like a little road. There were trees on one side and a drop off on the other side. Jack goes down, and he stops right at a curve in front of a tree. Buster goes next, and he starts going all crazy legs. Mel yells, 'Buster, slow down!' But he just kept going, evidently not knowing how to slow down. After yelling "SLOW DOWN" a couple of times, Mel yelled, 'Buster, FALL DOWN!'" But Buster didn't know how to fall down either. He crashed into Jack, and the two of them did a 360. By God's grace, they didn't go over the cliff or hit the tree. "Boy, were we relieved!" Vonnie says.

Colossians 2:7 continues to be a vital part of discipleship at Denton Bible. Anyone who desires to serve in a leadership position must complete the training. Discipleship took off at Denton Bible Church. However, sharing Christ and the excitement of conversions and baptisms limped along. Mel and Tommy wondered, "What are we going to do about that?" No ministries existed at DBC to equip people to share Christ. Mel heard about a program called *Evangelism Explosion (E.E.)* that taught people how to share the gospel. It was created by Pastor D. James Kennedy of Orlando, Florida. Mel called Kennedy's church office to see about starting *Evangelism Explosion* at Denton Bible Church. When Mel spoke with the secretary at

Kennedy's church, she explained, "Well, to start it in your church, you have to go through our training done by one of our people or somebody that we've already trained."

"Do you have one of those training sessions going on?" Mel asked.

She indicated a workshop was available in Dell City, Oklahoma. Mel registered three people to attend: Betty Ann McClung, Ken Metcalf, and Charles Stolfus. She asked if Mel was the pastor, and Mel said, "One of them."

"You have to come too," she said. Mel asked her if it made any difference if he had been through seminary.

"No," she replied. "We've found that if we try to start *Evangelism Explosion* in a church without the senior leadership behind it, it will probably fail. But if the top leadership in a church is behind *E.E.*, it will explode." Mel signed up for the week-long training in Dell City, Oklahoma with the others from DBC. They were there for six days and six nights. In the daytime, they received instruction and memorized the *E.E.* outline. In the evenings, they partnered with someone at the church who was trained in *E.E.* The guy who had experience knocked on doors and talked to people, while a couple of trainees listened and learned.

Mel came home from the six days in Dell City and visited his mother in Dallas where she lived with her widowed sister. Mel's mother asked, "Well, son, where have you been the past week?"

Mel said, "Mom, I'm glad you asked. Can I ask you a couple of questions?" He asked her the two diagnostic questions they learned for *E.E.* Mel's mom had taken him to church since he was at her knee, and he expected her to know the answers.

"Mom, if you died tonight, do you know where you would spend eternity?"

She replied, "I didn't understand that we could know we were going to heaven."

Then he told her, "The Bible says when we die, we're going to stand before God." Mel asked her the second question, "Why should God let you into His heaven?"

His mother thought for a little while, and then said, "Well, I was a good wife to your father before he passed away, and I tried to be a good mother to you children."

Mel was surprised. After hearing all those Baptist sermons, she had no idea about what it took to get to heaven. Mel went through the Evangelism Explosion outline with her, and at age eighty-six she prayed to receive Christ.

Mel's mother did not die of illness; she just got tired of living. She broke a hip and her pelvis, and she became totally bedridden. Unable to carry her to the bathroom or take care of her needs properly, Mel had to put her in a nursing home. It broke his heart. When Mel visited her, she would cry and ask him to take her home. Mel would cry too. Eventually, she stopped eating and drinking. When she died at the age of one hundred one and a half, Mel knew without a doubt that she was in heaven.

Mel, Charles, Ken and Betty Ann started Evangelism Explosion at DBC, and Denton Bible offered the classes for about twenty years. Mel and others called on people who visited DBC. Some people attending Denton Bible today continued coming because of those visitations. "Simply because we took time to go visit and show them that we really care," Mel notes.

In addition to structured discipleship programs, Mel was always open to innovative ways of discipling men and women—especially if it involved going back to his beloved Colorado. A new couple at Denton Bible Church would provide just such an opportunity.

Chapter 8

Backpacking, Skiing, and Beyond

Ron and Teri Patton will never forget July 4, 1976. They were walking near the historic courthouse on the Denton Square when a couple of college kids handed them a leaflet about Denton Bible Church. Some friends of the Pattons also mentioned Denton Bible Church, so Ron and Teri said, "Let's give it a try." They went the following Sunday to the United Ministry Center on the UNT campus where DBC met and heard Mel preach. The fledgling church could only meet for an hour, and then everyone had to leave. "We need more time," the college kids kept saying. After attending DBC for only four months, the Pattons offered their home as a meeting place.

Bedrooms became Sunday school classrooms. Ron says, "Have you ever tried to get rid of a bunch of college kids at noon?" The Pattons had three school age children at the time. One other family with children came, and some married couples with no children. The remainder of the congregation consisted of college students. Ron and Teri watched God grow Denton Bible Church from its humble beginnings to a church that reaches around the world through missionaries, pastors' training, women's training, and through in-house teaching materials.

Sometime in the 1980's, Mel and Ron began offering men's ski trips in the winter and backpacking trips in the summer. Mel gave Ron the responsibility of organizing the trips. "Fifteen or twenty of us would fly on Thursday night to the ski resort in Colorado," Ron says. "Some of the men wouldn't ski; they came for the fellowship. When women get together they open up quickly, but men aren't like that. It takes men a good twenty-four hours." Ron adds, "Over a period of a couple of days you'd see men start talking as they began getting close to one another." Ron remembers, "One guy said, 'I thought that man had the perfect marriage and family. I realized he's got the same problems I do.'"

As the men sat around the campfire, Tommy shared a message from the Bible. "Those trips were a real blessing," Ron says. On Sunday night, the men flew home, changed by loving one another, listening to one another, encouraging one another, praying for one another, and hearing God's Word. Denton Bible was implementing the "one another" principle Mel had learned from Dr. Getz at seminary.

A couple of times the men had father-son backpacking trips. Ron says, "It was great seeing the men out with their sons. We always went to the same place, Weminuche Wilderness, named after the Weminuche Indians." This wilderness area of 488,210 acres in southwest Colorado, managed by the United States Forest Service, is the largest of its kind in the state of Colorado. Ron remembers, "We'd catch the train in Durango, and it would let us off, and we'd go up the Elk Park Creek trail and camp about eleven thousand feet. Tommy would march up the trail memorizing Scripture. The next day we would take the boys up to the Continental Divide. The following day we'd come back and wave the train down and go back, so we were gone three days."

The men developed comradeship through shared experiences and laughter. One morning, Tommy got up and said, "Ronnie, how do you fix this?" He held up a package of dehydrated eggs.

"Well, Tommy, what does it say?" Ron asked.

"It says add hot water."

"So add hot water." Ten minutes later Ron looked around and saw Tommy eating out of the packet, "What are you doing?"

Tommy grimaced, "This is horrible."

"Tommy, you add water, and then you *cook* them."

A backpack trip changed the life of one little boy named Homer Adams, Jr. Mel says, "Early on in our ministry at DBC, Homer

Adams Sr. said, 'We're going to Israel, and we'd like to know if you'd be our guest. We'd like to pay for your trip.' Homer was a chiropractor in North Dallas, and his son, Homer Jr. was in Patty's kindergarten class at Trinity Christian Academy. Patty and I made eight trips together with the Adams, and I made an additional trip by myself with them."

In the late 1970's on one of the trips to Israel, Homer's wife, Kathy, asked Mel, "What are you guys doing this summer?"

Mel said, "Well, we're going on a backpacking trip to Colorado with the church. It's a wonderful trip for young people because it teaches them about discipline."

Homer and Kathy looked at Mel and said, "Would you do something for us? You know little Homer is our only child, and he's spoiled rotten. He's gotten anything he's ever wanted. Would you mind taking him on that backpacking trip and stretching him?"

Mel said, "Sure."

Mel explains what happened next, "We took little Homer—who was about seven years old at the time—with us. I don't know if he'd ever been separated from his parents for any length of time. We got on the train in Durango, Colorado headed toward Silverton. We were about an hour and a half outside Durango when the train stopped, and we took all our packs out of the baggage car. We put our packs on our back, and we started up the trail. We were going up about thirteen thousand feet on an established trail. We had gone about a hundred yards when Homer took off his pack, threw it on the ground, and said, 'I'm not carrying this stupid thing!'"

Mel continues, "'Well, Homer,' I said, 'that's your food and your bedroll. If you want to leave it here, that's fine, but we're going on up the trail.' Homer grabbed his pack and came with us, but we had to coax him all the way up. It was a strenuous trip, and Homer really got stretched. When we got back to the train station, he walked around like he'd conquered the world. When he arrived home, Kathy asked, 'What in the world did you do to this son of ours? He's competitive now and involved in activities.'" Mel adds, "Homer, Jr. grew up and followed in his dad's footsteps. He is a chiropractor in North Dallas, and he and his wife have five children." The lessons he learned on that backpacking trip with Mel likely contributed to his success today.

After years of watching Mel in situations like that with little Homer, Ron Patton reflects, "I learned how to be a man, not necessarily by him preaching to me, but by just observing him. He is also a great example of how a man should treat his wife. Mel has foresight and vision, like bringing in *Evangelism Explosion* and *2:7* in the early years of DBC." Both Ron and Teri love Mel. Teri says, "He's so humble. It's amazing with his accomplishments, through the Lord, of course, that he's such a humble man."

In the late 1980's, Mel heard about a man named Frank Tillapaugh who pastored Bear Valley Baptist Church in Denver, Colorado. Tillapaugh began a program called *Unleashing the Church* that peaked Mel's attention. Mel and Patty visited Tillapaugh to learn more. He came home and told Tommy and the elders, "You ought to go see him," They did. Tillapaugh emphasized getting the entire congregation of laypeople doing ministry, rather than assigning the fulfillment of Great Commission to the "professional" paid staffers. Tillapaugh also challenged churches to break out of the "fortress" mentality, expecting the unsaved to come into the church to hear the Gospel. He dared believers to carry the Gospel beyond the four walls of the church into the workplace, the parks, the neighborhoods, even the red-light-districts of our communities.

Because of visiting with Frank Tillapaugh, Mel preached a four-part series called "Unleashing the Church" in 1989. He put a vision before the congregation of using their gifts and talents to start new ministries. Denton Bible Church leadership decided every ministry of in-reach serving the church would be matched by a new ministry of out-reach into the community. Mel yearned for DBC folks to step out in faith and trust God to do great things.

Meanwhile, as Denton Bible Church grew, he and Tommy planted additional churches. Many people in Denton didn't want to attend an established church, so DBC started Church on the Square in a movie theater. Five men formed a leadership team to begin this ministry for the unchurched. John Bordeaux began as pastor, then Wayne Stiles, and later Bryan Collins. The congregation, called Denton Community Church today, is still led by Bryan.

When visiting his home church in Pueblo, Colorado, Mel discovered that the congregation wasn't doing well. Ron Chadwick, who discipled Mel, had returned to Pueblo. Ron, Mel and Travis Williams started a new church called Mesa Bible Church. Mel continued to plant churches after he retired, including one in the Vail, Colorado area. Several cities in Texas have Denton Bible church plants including Decatur, Sanger, Gainesville, Sherman, and Southlake. Another church began in St. Simons Island, Georgia. This congregation started from someone listening to tapes of Tommy's sermons.

In addition to planting churches, Mel and Tommy prayed for a youth pastor for Denton Bible. One day Mel walked in and told Tommy, "I think I met our future youth pastor today."

"Is that right? Who is it?"

Tommy was in for a surprise.

Chapter 9

High School Ministry Takes Off

M el divulged the name of the new youth minister, "Keith Chancey."

Tommy shook his head, "You'll never get him. He's deeply involved with KLIFE."

Keith tells of his first meeting with Mel. "My wife Karen and I felt like God was calling us from KLIFE, a parachurch ministry for teens and their families, to ministry in the church. We began praying diligently about where to go. A buddy of mine was the youth pastor at Northwest Bible Church in Dallas, so I visited him and told him what God had put on my heart. While I was talking to my friend about opportunities at several churches, Mel walked in and said, 'I'm looking for a youth pastor.' I don't know if my buddy even knew who this guy was, but Mel was adamant. His church needed a youth pastor."

Unknown to Mel, Tommy had spoken to the KLIFE staff a year earlier. KLIFE had four hundred kids in the program along with one hundred volunteers. Keith says, "When we walked out of that meeting, I asked Tommy if he'd disciple me. I never asked Tommy what he did for a living; I didn't know about Denton Bible Church. I was this young twenty-four-year-old kid in ministry, taking what I saw as a great commodity, and going, 'Teach me, teach me.' I drove to Denton and met Tommy at Grandy's. Eventually, I asked him if I could bring some of my buddies and move the meeting a little bit south."

This was the start of Young Guns, the nine-month disciple-ship program at DBC for guys in their twenties, before officially being named Young Guns. Keith remembers, "We had myself, Todd Wagner, who is now the pastor of Watermark Church, Kirk McJunkin, Athletic Director of Trinity Christian Academy, Kelly Shackleford, head of the Liberty Foundation, and Scott Polk, who helped start Watermark Church, James Stecker of Campus Crusade, and David Wills who worked with Focus on the Family. Like the L.A. Lakers' starting five, these guys—who are great in ministry today—began with Tommy."

When Mel spoke with Tommy about Keith joining DBC as youth pastor, Mel told Tommy, "Don't take 'no' for an answer." The advice was unnecessary; God had prepared Keith's heart to accept. Keith felt he needed to be at DBC because of Mel. "He didn't just see me, but he saw through me. He saw me not for who I was, but for who I could become," Keith says. "All he could do was talk about this church called Denton Bible Church. He sold me on the vision of how to equip men and women to be warriors for Christ. Mel had a vision for the church that I'd never seen a man have. He said, 'This is the fulfillment of the Great Commission. We've got to equip people, and we've got to send them around the world. Chancey, I'm going to send you places.'"

Keith went to Denton Bible Church, sight unseen. Keith says, "When I first started at DBC there were four kids in the junior high, high school, and college ministry. They put me in a room upstairs that used to be a missions closet in the Sumrall Center. I told them, 'You do know that you asked me to be the youth pastor. This isn't even a ministry you've got with four people.'"

Mel said, "Dream your dream."

Tommy asked, "Chancey, what do you see this ministry becoming?"

I said, "I see this ministry with over two hundred kids." At the time, there was only one hundred-fifty people in the church. Tommy slapped me on the forehead and called me Joseph. He said, "I'm calling you *The Dreamer*. You're seeing more kids than there are people in this church right now."

Keith says, "The youth ministry grew until we had 50, 100, 200, 400, then 600 kids. There wasn't a day that went by that Mel didn't give a word of encouragement and tell me how proud he was of me. But then he'd say, 'You know you have to send people. You have to send them to China.' Mel would always encourage, but then he would say, "Just keep dreaming the dream. Keep building this ministry, but keep sending people around the world."

Keith says, "The selflessness and humility of Mel Sumrall was one of the greatest lessons I've ever learned in my life. What I saw was a man who started DBC and then willingly said, 'Let Tommy be the pastor teacher, and let me be the shepherd of this congregation.' For a guy who chose to go to seminary at forty-eight years old to become equipped to teach, and to give that up and allow another man to take his position, is incredible. He did it because he saw Tommy's gifts as so unique. It's amazing to see a man who can see a vision, and it doesn't have to consist of himself," Keith says. "As soon as I got there, Tommy began taking over the full-time teaching ministry. Mel was teaching little bits and pieces at times, but he became the shepherd and did an incredible job. I learned 1 Corinthians 12 and Romans 12, the gifts of the Spirit, and how every person is unique in the body. Mel emphasized that more than anybody I've ever known. Mel is not a sideline coach. He gets involved in your life, and he wants to come check on you.

"Mel can't sit still. He had me, Margaret Ashmore, James Skinner, Bo Towns, we're going to Nepal, we're at Mt. Everest, we're in Pokura which is the furthest place from Kathmandu, the capital of Nepal. Mel, at seventy plus years old, was just going for it. He had the ability to fly that far, and to use whatever transportation was available, and to love everybody and to know everybody's name. And to hug, whether it was a Nepalese, or a Russian. Anybody he met, he always made feel special. Mel would go to the one thing he knew very, very well. He would go to the Word of God and teach the Word. Mel was always ready in-season and out-of-season to make sure people knew the value of the sword of the Spirit."

Keith says, "I learned from Mel never to be satisfied with people as they are. See them for who they could become and encourage them, develop them, train them, but most importantly give them a vision. What I do today with the Kanakuk Institute is a lot of what I saw Mel do. We train and send all around the world for the cause of Christ. As of now, we've sent over one thousand people around the world to make a difference for the cause of Christ.

"I never understood the church. Mel began to help me understand the Great Commission. That's when it all began to make sense. We are a sending agency. We're not going to make you comfortable. One thing Mel would always teach is that you can't be comfortable where you're at. You've got to get going where you need to be. For the very first time I learned what it was like for us as the body of Christ to help every person discover their gift set and to allow them to serve the body of Christ and to make Christ known. Mel was emphatic about making sure DBC was doing that. There's never a day that goes by that I don't think about how Mel Sumrall hugs people and loves people. It's the way I believe the body of Christ should be."

God calls the body of Christ to love those outside the church, and He was preparing the people of Denton Bible Church to reach out in an incredible way.

Chapter 10

Loving People Outside the Church Walls

As the youth ministry exploded, Mel and Tommy prayed about helping those in the community who need food, clothing, household goods, and house repairs. Tommy asked Mel, "Who do you think could do this?" Mel suggested Al and Tracie Jacobson. Al and Tracie originally joined Denton Bible Church in 1981 but left in 1986 for a job opportunity. On December 29, 1990, Tommy called them in Florida and asked them to return and head up a new ministry. Tracie remembers, "Al started crying, and I thought, 'Oh my gosh, somebody's died!'" Al says, "It was so touching that Tommy would call and ask us to do this. There was such a great need in the community."

As the Jacobsons moved back to Denton, Tommy launched this community outreach by preaching a series on giving. Ushers distributed cards during the sermon so people could write down their abilities, material provisions, and spiritual gifts which God could use in serving the community. Al says, "There were plumbers, electricians, gardeners, and people willing to help with food and clothing needs." Based on the information provided on the cards, Al and Tracie decided to focus initially on food, clothing and furniture.

Al had worked for a wonderful Christian homebuilder in Florida who called his construction company Vision Homes. Al got permission for DBC to use the name Vision Ministries. Tracie says, "That first year Vision didn't have a place to meet, so we did everything out of our house. Volunteers built a little chapel, where people dropped off donations." That little chapel now sits in the Denton Bible Church parking lot.

After a year, Vision Ministries moved from the Jacobsons' home to a facility on the Denton Square which they shared with a DBC church plant. "It was a good pairing," Tracie says, "because the people we served identified with Denton Community Church (DCC) which had a seeker's mentality." Some of the Vision volunteers built Sunday school rooms for Denton Community Church, and these doubled as consultation rooms for Vision during the week. Eventually, Vision moved from the Church on the Square to a former carpet store on Maple Street. "It was a huge place, and Al and the guys hung drywall, laid carpet and turned it into a usable space," Tracie says. Al's prior experience as a builder fit perfectly with Vision. As Al drove around Denton, he saw people standing in the rain waiting for a bus. Al and the volunteers built covered bus stops all over Denton. They also built wheelchair ramps and made house repairs. Eventually, construction needs outpaced Vision's ability to handle them.

Around 1993, the Sweat Team started as a spinoff from Vision Ministries with Dave Ferree managing it until 2010 when Wayne Carrigan took over. Volunteers with the Sweat Team help widows and those on fixed incomes with house repairs, wheelchair ramps, yard work, roofing, moves, and many other things. While acknowledging the importance of helping people with physical needs, Wayne and the Sweat Team volunteers recognize people need Jesus. As they work, they pray for opportunities to share the gospel.

Al reflects on how God prepared him and Tracie for Vision Ministries, "People who came with needs were ninety percent Hispanic. I was raised in Columbia with missionary parents until I was seventeen years old, so I spoke Spanish. Tracie's folks were missionaries in Cuba; she also spoke Spanish."

The Jacobsons retired from Vision Ministries when Al turned seventy years old, the mandatory age for retirement at Denton Bible Church. Al says, "I enjoyed the twenty years we served with

Vision; we have all positive memories. I'd do it all over again with no regrets."

Michael Pirtle and Carrie Powell now oversee Vision Ministries. Last year, Vision gave away 35,625 pounds of food, including several hundred pounds of meat from the Cattle Ministry at DBC. In addition, they issued 1,414 vouchers for clothing. Pat Smith serves as Director of Local Missions, overseeing Vision, Sweat Team, and Shiloh Field. Shiloh, the largest community garden in the country, was started by Gene Gumfory in 2009.

Reflecting on his relationship with Mel, Al says, "He never slowed down, and he never met a stranger. I've tried to imitate that and Mel's ability to meet people where they are. Mel was always ready to be involved where he felt God was working." Tracie appreciates that Mel has continually demonstrated the importance and power of prayer. Following Mel's example, she prays faithfully for Vision, missionaries, friends, family and those God puts in her path.

As Denton Bible Church continued growing and adding ministries, Mel and Tommy turned next to equipping women for the work of the ministry.

Chapter 11

Women's Ministry at Denton Bible Church

Before there was a formal women's ministry at Denton Bible Church, Teresa Nelson taught Bible studies for women. Ann Little, who served as Director of Women's ministries from 1998 to 2016, remembers coming to DBC in 1989. "When I moved here I didn't know anybody," Ann says. "I joined Teresa's group. Eventually, Teresa started the mom's group, and I started leading Bible studies."

A major milestone took place with women's ministries with the development of a foundational study called *The Titus 2 Woman*. Tommy credits Mel with starting all the programs at Denton Bible Church except *Titus 2*. Tommy asked Mel one day, "Who do you counsel most of the time?"

"About ninety percent of them are women, because guys are hesitant to come."

"Do you know anything about women?" Tommy asked.

"I've got three daughters, and I still don't know anything about women."

Tommy replied, "I've never had a sister. I don't have a daughter. I don't know anything about women. Titus 2 says older women are to train younger women. We're spending all our time with these women, and we don't have a clue." Mel and Tommy set up a meeting with the women in the church over the age of forty. They had a room full of women and figured there was something like three thousand years of experience in that room. Tommy told them, "We're going to put the responsibility for women on y'all."

Barbara McGee got together with Marquita Strader and a group of ladies, and they started working on *The Titus 2 Woman*. Barbara and Marquita wrote one chapter ahead of the ladies going through the study, and then passed out the mimeographed sheets the following week. In 1992, Linda Heydrick took the class and suggested putting the material in a permanent format. Marquita's health had declined, so Barbara and Linda worked on it together.

"*Titus 2* was well known throughout the church," Ann says. "The edited form was much easier to do." As *Titus 2* grew, so did other Bible activities for ladies such as retreats and mother-daughter teas. The first women's board consisted of Barbara McGee, Marquita Strader, Ann Little, Ethel Davidge, Teresa Nelson, Nellyne McFarlane, and Peggy Morgan.

Ann says, "Mel has always respected women, both at home and abroad. When he stepped down from staff and started traveling with Patty and teaching *Bible Training Center for Pastors (BTCP)*, he saw that women had influence as well as pastors. Mel encouraged the women at Denton Bible Church to go on mission trips and teach *Titus 2* in villages and in the bush. As they traveled to different countries, Mel and Patty recognized the need to teach women, perhaps the most neglected group of people in the mission field."

Ann continues, "*Titus 2* studies the roles of women and how to do relationships. It transcends cultures, making it extremely effective overseas. We were careful to remove illustrations or anything that would be confusing. It crossed cultural barriers. It showed women who they were, what their ministry was, and it gave them a ministry resource to help and train their women." *Titus 2* spread by word of mouth. As women moved from Denton, they would talk about *Titus 2* wherever they went. Orders came from churches around the country.

For Ethel Davidge, completing *Titus 2* was life-changing. Ethel and her husband Miller joined Denton Bible Church in 1985, Mel was teaching *BTCP* at Denton Bible Church and taking men around the world to teach it. Miller had completed *BTCP* and wanted to go with Mel, but he told Ethel, "I won't go unless you go with me." Their first trip was to India.

While Mel and Miller taught the men, Patty and Ethel invited the Indian women who served with Campus Crusade to join them in the hotel for tea and cookies. Ethel says, "There were about twelve ladies; they spoke English, but it was hard to understand them. We told them, 'This study was written by ladies in our church, and we brought it to see if it would meet any of your needs.' The topics in *Titus 2* are ones that touched their hearts because they're universal." Ethel thought, "If we go again, I'm bringing this study, and we're going to teach these ladies while the men are in the *BTCP* class."

After that first trip, Miller and Ethel traveled with Mel and Patty to Cambodia and Bangladesh where Ethel and Patty taught *Titus 2* to mainly Campus Crusade wives. In Cambodia it took only twenty-five minutes to gather one hundred and fifty women for Patty and Ethel to teach. Ethel recalls, "The first language that *Titus 2* was translated into was Myanmar (Burmese). The next one was Swahili in Kenya. The third one was probably Spanish, and the fourth one was Russian. People wanted to translate it into other languages, including Arabic." *Titus 2* is now available in ten languages and has been taken to over thirty countries.

As a senior, Ethel is still going strong. Through the years, Ethel witnessed Mel's example that God is never through with us, no matter how old we are. Ethel says, "The greatest lesson I learned from Mel is that God has a purpose and a plan for your life,"

God's plans for Mel and Tommy were changing. With Mel's encouragement, Tommy took on more of the preaching. God had another purpose for Mel.

Chapter 12

God Calls Mel and Patty to Missions

At age 62, Mel stepped down as senior pastor of Denton Bible Church. Mel and Tommy continued their close relationship as changes took place. Mel and Patty were in good health and zealous to continue serving God. As Mel prayed and thought about what to do next, Steve and Sarah Pogue came to mind. They joined DBC in 1986 and have served with CRU (formerly Campus Crusade for Christ) since 1977.

Steve recalls, "Mel called me, and he was thinking about the next stage of life. We went to lunch at a cafeteria, and he asked me, 'Is there anything I can do in connection with Crusade?' I knew that his life was about to change. I thought, 'If he gets involved, especially with Bill Bright being a peer, his life will never be the same.' Mel desires to reach the world—not just focus on one little part in Denton, Texas and one church. He has a global vision. I felt like he and Bill would have similar outlooks for the world and for discipleship. Both men want to involve other people in ministry. They don't build ministry around themselves. They don't draw attention to themselves. It was never Bill Bright's ministry; it was always Campus Crusade. Mel has done that, too. He started Denton Bible Church, and a lot of people probably don't know who he is. Mel and Bill are humble leaders and yet great visionary leaders, very directed leaders."

Steve relates the similarities between Bill Bright and Mel. "They were both born within a few years of each other in small towns. Both were business people. They both lived through the Depression and World War II. They both had this tremendous sense that God was going to use them to reach the world. According to Steve, Mel came along at the right time. Campus Crusade was showing the Jesus film around the world, probably the most shown film in the world. They hoped to start churches after showing the Jesus film. Today there are two million churches that have been planted around the world.

Mel went on what CRU called a "vision trip" to the Philippines. Jerry Sharpless, who worked with CRU's international ministries at their headquarters in Orlando, got Mel on that trip and connected him with Bill Bright. Bill spoke to a couple hundred Southeast Asia staff members. These people weren't Americans, but nationals from various countries like Nepal, Bangladesh, Thailand, Burma, Malaysia, Philippines and Indonesia. During Bill Bright's speech, he mentioned CRU's goal of starting a million churches in the next ten years. Mel asked the question, "Who's going to train the pastors?" They had no plans for doing that. Mel said that Bill Bright was probably the most single-minded man he ever met, other than Tom Nelson. Tommy's all about preaching; Bill Bright was all about winning the world for Christ. "That's what God called him to do, and that's what he should do," Mel said. But Mel saw a need to train the leadership in all the start-up churches. Many pastors around the world have never received any formal training.

Steve comments, "Once CRU had that connection with Mel, once they understood who he was and what he offered, then it's like, 'This is going to be a great, ongoing relationship.' Mel and Patty had the vision and commitment to go into some very difficult places in the world; places where there aren't any amenities that most Americans would consider essential. They'd go and minister and often get ill because the conditions were so bad. Then they'd come home, recuperate, and then go somewhere else in the world. Some of the greatest impact of Denton Bible Church is in places like Nepal and other areas of Asia where Mel and Patty have had a significant influence. We won't necessarily know about that here in the United States, but they have certainly had a huge impact in those places."

"Mel had the experience and the vision to come alongside churches and start training pastors, eventually using *Bible Training Center for Pastors (BTCP),*" Steve says, "Churches need great leaders. It's important and critical. Great leadership comes from being trained in the Scriptures more than having a formal seminary education. The person who understands the authority of God's Word, looks to the Bible, and is a humble leader, then fulfills the very essence of *BTCP*—not to be a dictator, but to be a shepherd in a church."

Mel came home from the conference with Bill Bright in the Philippines and received calls from Crusade national directors in Southeast Asia. He taught leadership conferences in Nepal, Bangladesh, Thailand, Burma, Malaysia, Philippines, Indonesia and others, always taking Patty with him. Mel was doing a leadership conference with pastors in Nepal, and he thought, "What am I going to talk to these guys about. I don't know their background, never seen them, don't know what they had." He was teaching the life of Christ and happened to mention the second coming of Christ. A hand went up. Mel nudged his translator, Prakash Subba, and asked him to find out what the question was. Prakash Subba said, "They want you to say more about the second coming of Christ; they've never heard anything about that." Encounters like this cemented Mel's thinking about the great need to train church leadership around the world. He thought about Bill Bright's goal to start a million churches. "Who's going to train the pastors to lead the churches?" Mel thought again. "This has got to be the greatest need in the mission field."

Mel struggled to find any material on the market in 1987 that he could use to train pastors. Mel had been doing the leadership conferences for a few years when he got a call from Tom LeBoutilier, one of the men he had discipled. Tom was a captain with American Airlines, and he said, "Hey, can you come down to Atlanta?" Tom, who was single at the time, told Mel, "Come down and we'll do a fish fry for the singles at First Baptist." This happened to be Charles Stanley's church.

Mel and Patty went to the fish fry in Atlanta, and while there, Mel talked with Randy Gardner, the singles pastor. Mel told him that the big problem with training pastors in other countries was the lack of available materials. Randy told him, "You need to talk to Dennis Mock." Dennis Mock had been an attorney for thirteen years until the Lord changed his life. He left the practice and went to Dallas Seminary. When he graduated, he went to work writing materials for Charles Stanley. Charles Stanley was scheduled for ministry work in Africa, but at the last minute he couldn't go. He asked Dennis to take his place.

Dennis agreed, but said, "I don't want to do evangelism. I'd rather train leadership." Charles Stanley responded, "Well, we can arrange that."

In Africa, Dennis spent three weeks training thirty-five to forty pastors. He was amazed at the desperate need for training. He returned and told Dr. Stanley, "We've got a big problem. There's no material on the market. Dr. Stanley replied, "I'll pay your salary for two years to develop some." Dennis Mock spent the next two years developing ten separate books covering the areas in which a pastor needed training. He called it *Bible Training Center for Pastors.*

After hearing about Dennis Mock, Mel asked Randy, "Where's Dennis now?"

"He's in Africa."

"You have a phone number?"

"Yeah."

Mel called Dennis Mock in Africa, and they talked. Mel wanted to check out the materials. Dennis said, "Come on down to Atlanta, and when I get back, we'll talk." When Dennis and Mel met, Dennis told him, "Take the material and use it to train pastors in Asia. I don't expect to get out of Africa." Mel told Dennis that he'd continue using the name, *BTCP* and follow any guidelines Dennis had. Denton Bible Church would not be connected to First Baptist or Dr. Mock with staff or money. Dennis said, "Sounds good to me."

Later, Mel traveled with Dennis to Mombasa, Kenya, which is about 99.9% Muslim. They met a young man working with Muslims. After Mel came home, he heard on the news about a missionary in Mombasa who had been attacked on the road. His wife was killed, and he was in the hospital for about a year recovering from the attack. It was the young man he and Dennis had met. Mel and Dennis also traveled together to Russia, India, the Philippines and several other places. Dr. Mock started a church in Atlanta specifically for raising funds for *BTCP*. Unlike Mel, he pursued training pastors in America where thirty-three percent of Baptist pastors lacked formal theological training. Dr. Mock developed a vibrant ministry to these pastors while Mel concentrated on training pastors overseas. *BTCP* continues its mission of training pastors around the world. Dr. Mock is Chairman of the Board of Directors of *BTCP*, and Randy Gardner serves as President.

At one point, Mel and Patty went to Madrid, Spain which at the time had about forty-three million people with approximately two hundred thousand true believers. Almost all of them attended churches pastored by women. Mel went to Spain to train pastors, but not women pastors. He knew he couldn't change the culture, so he changed the name from *Bible Training Center for Pastors* to *Bible Training Center for Leaders (BTCL)* and taught the women. He eliminated a couple of the books in the course including *Expository Preaching*. Dr. Mock agreed that was the right thing to do. Mel says, "Are you going to have women pastors who know the word of God and can teach people, or are you going to have women pastors who don't know the word of God but are teaching anyway?"

Steve Pogue notes, "Mel sees needs and sees how God could work in these needs, and what God can do. That has been consistent throughout his life." Steve also shares evidence that Mel's commitment is to people, not merely a program. He states, "Mel cared for Patty until the very end. There was a graduation for *Bible Training Center for Leaders* and *BTCP* at Denton Bible Church about a month before Patty passed away. Mel sat with me at the back. They were getting towards the end of it, and they were going to recognize Mel. Mel had already told me, 'I have to go take care of my sweetie.' They were going to applaud him, yet he had already gone home to take care of Patty. He kept his priority taking care of Patty."

Asked what Mel means to him personally, Steve replied, "He's a great example. Some of the people I admire most in leadership are not necessarily those who appear to be as dynamic as others. They don't appear to be out front, yet they're leading in a very humble, dynamic way year-after-year. Mel has been very consistent. You go to his house, and he has one or two Bibles open, he has hymns playing. There's still this sense of wanting to keep the Lord at the center of his life. Ultimately, anything we want to do in missions must flow out of our walk with the Lord. We don't want the ministry to replace our devotion to the Master."

As Mel began teaching *BTCP* in Southeast Asia and around the world, he took a young man with him whose heart for the world beat like Mel's. Little did this young man know that God was about to open doors that would thrust him into his lifetime calling.

Chapter 13

Step Up, Young Man!

James Arnold was saved, but he was running from God. After coming back to the Lord, James's focus changed entirely. He had been pursuing a business degree, but for all the wrong reasons. James replaced his old plans with new goals. In 1988 he moved to Denton to attend grad school at UNT to study physiology. He wanted to get a Ph.D. so he could be a university professor and tell people about Jesus.

James says, "I got here, and the first thing I did was get involved with Campus Crusade at UNT. I asked around for the best church in town. Everyone said, 'Denton Bible.' So, that's where I went. Denton Bible was meeting at the Sumrall Center with a few hundred people. I realized Mel was the guy behind Denton Bible, so I went to Mel's home, walked up the sidewalk, and knocked at the door. Patty opened the door, and I asked if Mel was there. He was, and I asked him if he liked to disciple men.

"Mel and I became buddies. He put me under a guy named Dino Roseland, our small groups pastor at the time. Dino was doing some things in Mexico, so I started leading college groups down to Mexico. At that point, I did everything at DBC related to missions. This was before Denton Bible had an actual missions department. Under Mel's tutelage, things kind of came to a convergence. I was about a year into my Master's in physiology and realized what I really wanted to do was tell people about Jesus. I went ahead and finished my Master's, but I also started DTS.

"Mel began dragging me around the world. Then, he put me in charge of missions to Mexico, and in 1990, I led a team to Russia. In 1994, I finished DTS for the first time with a Master of Arts. I went in pursuing a Master of Theology (Th.M.), but Mel said, 'I need you on staff.'"

From 1988 to 1994, James was in DBC missions in an unofficial capacity. He slept on the floor at the Sumrall Center so he could wake up at 2 a.m. to call Bangkok (this is before the Internet) to set up trips for Mel and himself. While in grad school, he was working for Mel forty hours a week. He was also working at the university teaching classes to make ends meet. In 1994, he joined the staff at Denton Bible Church on partial support at eight hundred dollars a month. James married Jen Wez in 1996 and returned to DTS to start picking away at his Th.M. He officially served as missions pastor at DBC from 1994-2007. James comments, "I was missions pastor for thirteen years, but titles were never an issue for Mel and me. It was like, 'You do this, I do that.' Maybe it was because Mel never had to question my respect or my loyalty. Mel's got flaws; he's not perfect. But he covered my flaws, and I covered his flaws."

James became Mel's boss for a few years. James comments, "It sounds bizarre, but that's Mel. I built an office for him, and the day the office was complete he came up with a nameplate and put *my* name on *his* door. That was him. I still live by his creed. 'If you can get someone else to do what you're doing, get them to do it, and you go do something else.'"

James and Mel went everywhere together. "Patty was always there taking care of us. I don't think I ever traveled with Mel without Patty. The next three to six months, we went to fifteen countries. Within ten years *BTCP* was translated into twenty languages, and now Denton Bible keeps about ten thousand men and women on rotation in about thirty countries worldwide. That's all from Mel climbing the mountain. Once I left home with twenty-seven plane tickets in my pocket. I was going through Russia, the Ukraine, India, Indonesia, Malaysia, and the Philippines. That was my docket the first two years I came on staff. I was in the United States seventy days in a two-year period. To date, I've visited is more than eighty countries.

"Mel had this vision: we need to train pastors. We started off in southeast Asia, India, Thailand, Cambodia, Nepal, the Philippines and various places throughout that region. As we traveled, we started getting into other places like Russia. For a year, I went to live in Costa Rica to open up all of South America. We never really got too deep into Africa, because Dr. Mock and his crew did that.

"The greatest lesson I've learned from Mel is give your life for Jesus. From that comes about a billion other lessons. Jesus is the priority. Keep Him as the priority and live accordingly. Fear not; don't worry about death in this world. Just go. He's gone to places that are not the safest places. His life has been in danger."

James adds, "I've also learned from Mel how to be a faithful husband. He would buy dresses for Patty, and it was always a great selection. She loved it! How many husbands would go dress shopping for their wives? She was always sweet. As Patty's health declined, he kept her at home and took care of her until she passed away on June 22, 2017. At Patty's memorial service, we heard testimony about Patty never raising her voice. Mel never raised his voice to Patty. I can't even remember a time when he was frustrated with Patty, even in the days when she wasn't altogether functioning. Mel would say, 'This is my honey, and I wait for her, and I go at her speed.' He took that verse literally, 'Husbands, love your wives as Christ loved the church,' (Ephesians 5:25). They're great examples, both of them. Patty was the example of what I wanted to marry when I was a single guy."

"Mel was always, 'Let's go see how the Bible works in the real world.' We would go fishing, and anytime the fish weren't biting Mel would say, 'Let's go find a church.' We would find a church, and Mel would ask them, 'What are you guys doing?' Then he would tell them about *BTCP*. Anywhere Mel went fishing, you have a *BTCP* center."

James says, "I would have swum the ocean to get back to the States for Patty's funeral on June 26, 2017. The world will stop for Mel Sumrall."

Mel's parents

Patty – 5 years old

Mel – 12 years old

Mel & brother Jerry

Mel the Marine

Mel & Patty – wedding

Patty on honeymoon

Mel graduates from University of Colorado

Mel the businessman

Mel – House he built in CO

Ron & Sally Chadwick – Mel's discipler

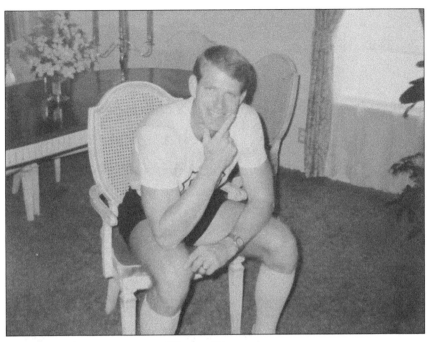

Young Tommy

Tommy & Teresa

Mel the skier

Tommy, Teresa, Ben, John – Clearing the land

Dedicating the land

Mel & Tommy – Wedding at Methodist church

Bill & Vonette Bright

Howard Hendricks (Prof) and wife Jeanne

Backpacking in Colorado

Mel loves fishing!

Mel with young Susan, Laura, Jerry

Mel and son Jerry fishing

Mel's mom – 100th birthday

Ski trip – first 2:7 class

Keith Chancey – first youth pastor

Al & Tracie Jacobson – First Vision Ministries directors

Mel in Nepal with Damerdar

Mel teaching in Asia

Mel teaching in India

Mel drinking out of coconut

Patty with African women

Patty teaching – mission field

Patty on mission field

Charles Stolfus in Thailand 2001

Margaret Ashmore on mission field

Michael Martin with Mel & Patty

Mel & James Arnold

Mel, Patty, Dan Heffley, Jack Manes, Warren Nystrom

Mel & Patty in Russia

Mel & Patty at Golden Triangle – S.E. Asia

Mel with Dennis Mock (far right)

John Brown, Bryan Collins, Mel & Patty

Mel & Patty with Mother Teresa

Mel with grandkids

Ann Little – Women's Ministry

Current SERVE staff

Mel & Gene Getz

Mel with disciples Cary Hull & Alan Chamberlain

Current staff – Denton Bible Church

Mel teaching widows on heaven

Mel with Millennials class

Adult Sumrall children (Karen, Laura, Susan, Jerry)

Patty in Mel's lap 2012

Mel and Patty in DBC foyer

Wall of DBC missionaries

Optimist Gym – Early meeting place

Sumrall Center

Current DBC sanctuary

Chapter 14

Sending Forth

As the demand for *BTCP* grew around the world, Mel realized he needed men to lead the graduates when they finished the course. Mel came up with a plan: train the elders and leaders at Denton Bible Church and send them out to teach *BTCP*. This was a novel idea for most of these men, but that didn't stop Mel from pushing them out of their comfort zone. People who hang around Mel better count on being challenged! The following stories of some of the men and women Mel sent around the world to teach *BTCP* and *BTCL* are not just stories of mission trips, but stories of richer lives. The lessons Mel instilled in these men and women shaped who they are today.

Jack Manes

Jack served as an elder at Denton Bible Church for twenty-five years. Mel assigned Jack Manes to Europe, Romania and that area. He made thirteen trips, including three to Russia, five to Romania, and one to Spain for a *BTCP* graduation and to teach book six of *BTCP*. He also made two trips to Venezuela, and one to Thailand.

On one of the evangelistic trips to Romania, Jack visited nearly every city and county in the country except Transylvania. He taught a class where it was -22 °F. It was snowing hard, but all the participants came. Jack comments, "If I hadn't been going on these trips and teaching, I would have been doing something negative. I discovered that the hearts and souls of people were the same. The first trip I made to Russia I cried for six months every time I talked about it. The Russians had been indoctrinated to think that all Americans are bad. Our interpreters weren't interested in spiritual things, but they saw Americans in a way they had never seen before. It was a life-changing experience for me and for them."

Warren Nystrom

Warren served on the elder board from 1996 to 2008. Mel sent Warren to Central America in the early 1990's to teach. Warren says, "The big trip was in 1998. Mel and Patty took Jack Manes, Dan Heffley, and me to Venezuela to learn how to teach *BTCP* and to get a handle on what was going on. Mel taught us how to relate to people in a foreign country, to listen to them, and to work through an interpreter."

In Valero, Venezuela, the DBC team worked with three pastors: Hipolito, Rojas, and Cesar. Warren recalls, "Many of the pastors in Venezuela couldn't go to seminary. Going through *BTCP* was like going to seminary because it covered all the aspects a pastor needed. You could see nationals in the *BTCP* courses bonding, and their friendships would cause excitement among them. 'We can do this; we can do this!' they said. Those attending were pastors from churches that were scattered around the country, not just guys in one church in Valencia or Valera."

According to Warren, Mel can perceive the various gifts and talents others possess. "Mel lit the fuse, and God blew it up. Mel told us before we took *BTCP*, 'You're going through this to do something with what you learn. You're not going to sit on it; I'm going to give you some assignments.' Knowing our backgrounds, Mel saw what people like Dan and I could do, with the power of God, things that we never thought possible. Mel would say, 'Pray about it, but also let God show you His strength in your life with the abilities He's given you.' Mel constantly challenged us. He pushed us out of our comfort zone. Working with Mel, you start to realize God will give you power to do things that He knew you could do. Mel gave me the opportunity to share my testimony on a Christian radio station in Kenya. Mel gave Dan and I different opportunities wherever we went."

Warren was eventually assigned to Venezuela. "I had gotten to know the pastors, and I taught *BTCP* there seven or eight times. It's a big country, and I traveled all over the country to do the classes. Mel told us, 'Take somebody with you so he can learn how to teach *BTCP.*' I did that with several guys. I would assign certain sections of *BTCP* to them so they would get used to teaching. The three pastors, Hipolito, Rojas, and Cesar oversaw *BTCP* in their area. "We eventually removed ourselves," Warren says, "and left them in charge. We can no longer go to Venezuela because it's illegal and dangerous; however, the work in Venezuela's still going on. I've Skyped with Cesar. Over a thousand pastors have been trained in *BTCP.*"

Mel taught the men to share the Scriptures. Warren says, "Mel told us, 'we're not there to lecture. We're there to share in a soft voice what the Lord has done and to use the Bible.' I would read a passage and have the interpreter point to it so the men would see that the source was the Word of God and not me. Mel emphasized the importance of that."

Mel also stressed the critical need to pray for the trip regarding safety and for teaching ability. He instructed the men to pray before teaching and to model prayer in their own lives. Realizing the importance of prayer, Warren and his wife, Ina, intercede for the short-term mission trips and career missionaries Denton Bible supports. Warren says, "By the time you get through praying for them, the morning is gone." DBC supports almost a hundred missionaries whose pictures hang in the church foyer.

Warren also appreciated the example Mel set by having Patty accompanying him on the trips. "It was important for my wife Ina to see that she too could go overseas and be involved in teaching," Warren says. "Ina went and taught quite a few times. When Ina came, we walked together and talked together and smiled together. The nationals saw our relationship. We were a demonstration to other couples of how God could use them together."

Dan Heffley

"We first came to Denton Bible in September 1987," Dan says. "I met Mel early on, because he was so outgoing and hugging everybody. I was sixty years old when I went on my first mission trip to Russia around 1993. I had retired early from the telephone company, and that allowed me to do mission work. After Russia, I went to Venezuela with Global Missions Fellowship (GMF) which partnered with Denton Bible Church. Jim Hill presented *BTCP* on that trip.

"Warren, Jack Manes, and I returned later to Valencia and Valero, Venezuela with Mel to learn how to present *BTCP*. Mel also assigned us a chapter in a book on discipleship that we were supposed to teach, but we never got around to it; however, I left my notes with one of the pastors. Several years later, someone from DBC went to Venezuela and talked to this pastor. He told them to tell me, 'Thank you so much for that material, because it's been used ever since for discipling.' That was a great encouragement.

"After that training trip, Mel assigned Warren to Venezuela, and I was assigned the rest of South America. From 1995 to 2015, I went to Argentina, Ecuador, Peru and Chile to start *BTCP*. My wife Bernice came with me several times and taught *Titus 2*. Bernice and I, with elder Dick Craven and his wife Virginia, visited Ecuador to do premarital counseling. Dick and Virginia also accompanied me to Venezuela to do premarital counseling. Besides South America, I went to Russia four times."

From Mel, Dan learned faithfulness, a love for the Lord, and a desire to be a witness. Dan served on the elder board for eighteen years before stepping down to take care of his ailing wife. Sadly, she passed away in 2017. Now, in his eighties, Dan once again serves as an elder at Denton Bible Church. Mel's early beliefs in Dan's gifts and abilities continues to produce fruit.

Charles Stolfus

Looking at Charles Stolfus now, a person might struggle to imagine him as an audacious, risk-taker tramping through jungles as a missionary in the '90s. When Charles was a thirty-eight-year-old single, Mel sent him to Thailand and other countries to teach *BTCP*. "I was very adventuresome as a single guy. I'd do anything, go anywhere," Charles says. "My life up to that point had been eclectic. I was a semi-truck driver, I rebuilt diesel engines on a road crew, I drove graders and dump trucks, built concrete fences, did teaching and college teaching."

Getting involved in missions sounded like fun, but Charles discovered it's not all fun on the mission field. He recounts his first trip to Thailand. "It was pretty scary. I was out in the middle of nowhere in the jungle. We'd fly from Bangkok and get a puddle jumper to Khomken, then drive to an encampment in the north part of Thailand near the Makong River. The places where I stayed consisted of four walls, a concrete slab, and a thatched roof. We slept on the concrete floor. There was no running water, so to get clean we scooped water onto our heads out of a thirty-five gallon trash can and let it run down our body."

Many times, in his early days of going on mission trips, Charles would ask himself, "Man, why am I here? Why am I doing this?" He remembers thinking, "It's hot and humid. You're lonely, tired, and uncomfortable. You've got greasy hair, can't take a shower, and the food sometimes makes you sick. Then I'd look at the audience of forty pastors without any training who were now learning *BTCP*. These men came from all over the country to the Khomken region, and they were the reason Charles returned again and again. "Sometimes it's not fun or exciting. It can be hard and discouraging, but I saw the hunger in these men to learn the Word of God. It truly transformed me."

Charles had some life-changing experiences. One time in the Philippines he stopped on a street corner jammed with twenty-five people. Without prior notice or preparation, he just started preaching. Charles says, "I stood there in the heat and humidity, and sweat poured off me. Sweat ran down my arms, my fingers. It was that hot. Sweat ran down my face onto my open Bible. Having to preach and encourage and challenge in those circumstances is difficult. I starting thinking, 'In many cases, this is what pastors in the rest of the world do every day, their whole lives.' It stuck in my mind and heart."

Sometimes funny or unusual things happened. Charles remembers a time in the jungle when it was raining like crazy. Chairs were placed on a concrete slab about the size of a basketball court. There were no walls, but there was a roof suspended by poles on each of the corners. "We were getting ready to teach, and I opened my notebook on the podium, and this large lizard jumped out at me." Charles adds, "That was a surprise!" Later, Charles was waiting to teach while a brother was leading in prayer. A big flying insect landed on the seat in front of one of the guys in the audience. "He reached out his hand and grabbed it and popped it in his mouth and ate it."

Charles ate his share of strange things. On one of his trips to Thailand, some men wearing headlamps and carrying flintlock rifles went into a sugar cane field. They shot a rat, which is considered a delicacy there. Charles comments, "They grilled it and served it up. It tasted really good. It's kind of a dark, greasy meat, but really flavorful." Another time, he was served a frog that had not been gutted. It was cut open and grilled with all the innards right there; he ate it. Charles was also served a salad with ants on top. On a trip with Jim McDonald, an elder at DBC, they were served a grilled moth. Both of them ate it. Charles says, "It tasted like peanut butter."

Mel adds, "Charles was still single then. He didn't have good sense."

Charles dealt with loneliness during those long stretches serving in the jungle. "I'd teach six or eight hours a day. The translators were tired after that, and they don't want to talk, and there was no one who understands English." Charles relates a story of how God came close to him in his loneliness. "I was single and getting older. I was wondering what God was up to. I felt like I could hardly buy a date and God had set Himself against me. Of course, that wasn't what God had done, but we feel that way sometimes. On one of the trips to Thailand. I couldn't sleep. I went out on the front porch of this little hut where I was staying. It was pitch black, and my hut was about a hundred yards away from where everyone else was staying. It was probably 3 a.m., and I was looking up into the darkness. I prayed, 'God, if You're there, would you show me?' It was a simple statement of a lonely single. I sat down with my eyes closed, when I sensed someone in front of me. I opened my eyes, and one of the Thai pastors had gotten up in the middle of the night. He couldn't have known I was awake, because there was no light in my hut. He had a bowl of fruit, and he gave it to me and went back to his hut. God prompted that pastor who couldn't even speak English and hardly knows me, to get up, get a bowl of fruit, bring it a hundred yards away, and give it to someone he didn't know would be there. It seems like a small thing, but those things change us."

God has shaped Charles through mission trips, and he encourages everyone to go on a short-term trip. However, many Christians won't go. Charles says, "We are unwilling to be inconvenienced. Or, we're too timid or fearful. Or, we lack initiative to venture out somewhere we've never been before or that's uncomfortable. We want God to use us to make a difference in the world, but we don't want to walk the path to see that happen. When I look back on my life, it's those situations that have transformed me. At times it's been hard and uncomfortable, but many times exciting and exhilarating.

"On one of my trips to the Philippines, myself and another guy rafted up a river, and there was this massive waterfall roaring down into the widened part of the river. We're in the middle of the jungle. We can't buy that kind of memory. It changes us to experience other parts of the world, to see the variety that God gave us on this planet, to see the variety of individuals."

Charles remembers a pastor in Thailand who was uneducated. He was the pastor because he had a Bible. His theology was rather messed up, but he had memorized dozens and dozens of verses, including obscure verses in the middle of Isaiah or Psalms. "We were teaching through Old Testament Survey, and every time we'd get to a verse where I would read it out loud or ask someone else to read it, this guy would stand up and recite it from memory. I marveled at this uneducated, untrained individual who nonetheless had spent significant amounts of time with God. That's amazing."

Asked what we can learn from other people and churches around the world, Charles replies, "The one thing that stands out is suffering. The American church hasn't had to suffer. Since our founding, we have been the blessed recipients of a long legacy of godly men and women, from the Puritans to the Pilgrims on through the colonial era into the Twentieth and Twenty-first Century. We have been blessed by freedom of worship, and Christians have had a voice in society. Increasingly, however, we're seeing that we're not in the majority. We're not favored. In many ways, we're condemned as bigots and seen as backward, judgmental, harsh, and putting our views on a level of denying the Holocaust or racism.

"It shocks me, and I've been convicted by the Lord that persecution is coming to the American church. Persecution has already come to many parts of the world, but they have found a way to thrive during suffering. I think America is going to have to learn from our brothers and sisters in Libya, Sudan, Egypt, Iraq, Syria and other places. We're going to have to learn, 'How does one thrive when you're the disfavored, and you're locked up in jail? When you're beheaded on the beach like they were in Libya?'"

Because Mel had the vision to send elders and staff around the world to teach *BTCP*, Charles experienced life-changing moments on the mission field. Charles says of Mel, "He is exemplary in so many ways. It's his life, his heart, his mind, his accomplishments. He's a very smart, bright individual. God used all of that to prepare Mel for the radical redirection of his life from the business world into ministry, and not at a young age. I'm sure in one sense it was like Paul stepping foot on the continent of Asia and stepping off into the darkness and saying, 'I don't know what's out there, but I know God will be with me.' Mel's life is an example of that. He went off to seminary and graduated and started a new church.

"We have a funny saying around Denton Bible Church: 'Mel has a wonderful plan for your life.' He's a visionary. He can see what others don't see. He's got courage to step out knowing that God is with him. He's got creativity and the social graces that enable him to develop relationships along the way that open doors and make possible the impossible. He takes a seed that was planted elsewhere, and he waters it, and it grows into something magnificent. Look at *BTCP*. He took that program, and through his leadership, it's been translated into dozens of languages. It's been taken to China, Egypt, Mongolia, Southeast Asia, Africa, South America, and Europe. That's exemplary in the best sense of the word.

"Mel's love for his wife was exemplary. He was always so gracious, so kind and tender when he referred to his bride. Watching Mel trust God when he encounters difficult things has made a huge impression on me. He's gone through difficult times at Denton Bible and had to make difficult decisions that a lot of people never heard about. He's endured disappointments and had successes that didn't go to his head. He's always given God the glory and other people the credit for his successes."

Charles remembers a statement made by Ronald Reagan, "It's amazing how much can get done when you don't care who gets the credit." Charles applies this to Mel, "Many, many times Mel's strategic vision and voice have been so critical and influential, and yet he didn't care if someone else got the praise, glory or whatever. It truly is amazing how much can get done when one doesn't care who gets the credit.

"One of my favorite verses in the Old Testament is Isaiah 66:2, and it's Isaiah quoting God, *'To this one I will look, to him who is humble and contrite, or broken of spirit, and who trembles at My word.'* God looks to that kind of individual. That's Mel. Humble, contrite of spirit, and who trembles at God's word."

Charles offers this personal note to Mel: "I love you, Mel, because of who you are and how God made you. The impact you've had on so many hundreds of thousands of people over the years astounds me!"

Mel not only impacted people around the world but also poured into people at Denton Bible Church. God has used Mel to change lives in radical ways, and now those people are pouring into others. The seeds Mel planted over the years continue to produce much fruit.

Chapter 15

Changed Lives

S tories of changed lives abound at Denton Bible Church. Through the years, God has used Mel and Tommy to encourage, inspire, and challenge people. Here are just a few of the people whose lives have been changed through their influence.

Michael Martin

God used Mel and Tommy to shape Michael Martin into the person he is today. Mike grew up in Buckner Children's Home after being taken away from his family. His father was in prison, and his brother was a habitual criminal who eventually died. When Mike was old enough to leave Buckner, he did so cussing his housemother on the way out. He joined the Marines and went to Okinawa where he picked up a black belt in karate. After his discharge from the Marines, Mike enrolled at UNT.

Tommy remembers seeing him around campus. "He had a blue toboggan on the back of his head. His voice was low, but he didn't talk much. He was just ominous. He trained in karate in front of Kerr Hall with Tom Severn who was number one in the world in karate." Tommy was speaking at McConnell Hall at UNT for Campus Crusade for Christ. He saw Mike sitting on a window ledge. Tommy thought, "He's going to kill me and eat me." But Mike was listening. Denton Bible Church was meeting at the Optimist Gym, and a few weeks later Tommy looked up and saw Mike in the service. "Everybody was kind of nervous with him there. But I got to know him, and he was just a seeking, gentle soul." Mike prayed to trust Christ as his Savior at UNT during a Campus Crusade conference.

"Mike has been a fixture at Denton Bible Church since 1977," Tommy said. He's passionate about apologetics and sharing the gospel. He became an Arlington cop so he could share the gospel with Hispanic kids."

Mike graduated from Dallas Seminary in 1992. "He worked his way through school by going to Oklahoma on fight night for boxing matches," Tommy said. "He has no cartilage in his nose because he's been busted up so many times. I bet he's been in ten thousand fights."

Mike currently serves in South Korea with Cadence International where, until recently, he served for seven years as director of Shalom House, ministering to soldiers from Camp Casey and Camp Hovey, both part of 2nd Infantry Division. He taught several weekly Bible studies, hosted a weekly movie night with home-cooked meals, took monthly trips to Seoul with troops for outreach to The Baby Box, an orphanage and practical ministry to the homeless in Seoul. He has now relocated to Camp Humphreys, Korea, where he will serve with the same goal in mind of discipling soldiers by wedding heart, head, and hands together.

Every Christmas, Mike calls Tommy from South Korea or wherever he is and starts the conversation by singing, "I'll have a blue Christmas without you." Tommy says, "Mike loves me, loves Teresa, loves Mel, loved Patty. He's as loyal to Denton Bible as anyone has ever been. Mike was a Marine, and Mel was a Marine, so they became close."

Once, Mike met Mel and Patty in Manila, Philippines in the 1990s. He says, "We found ourselves on one of the streets looking for a place to eat. We were waiting for a bus or taxi, and I saw this little boy about nine or ten years old sitting on the curb applying a tree leaf to the bottom of his foot. As soon as I mentioned it to Mel and Patty, Mel directed me to go across the street and get some gauze and antiseptic medicine. He suspected the young boy was applying a local remedy to an injured foot. When I got back, supplies in hand, there was Patty kneeling down next to the boy washing his feet with a wet handkerchief. I think it was dear Patty who then dressed and bandaged his foot up."

Mike recalls the big smile the little boy had on his face when he looked up at them, his foot now covered in white gauze. Mike found himself at the same spot the next day. He says, "That kid was reading a little evangelical pamphlet (in Tagalog) I'd handed him the day before. We entered a store, and I loaded him up on a lot of candy and a Coke. I didn't see him again but wouldn't be surprised if he had that bandage hanging up in his room at home, if he even had a home."

As a young man, Mike noticed the way Mel addressed young college girls. Mike says, "I hadn't been at Denton Bible Church long before I heard Mel calling young college girls 'Sweetheart' or 'Dear.' He did this in front of Patty, who didn't wince at all. It seemed odd to me, but I just chalked it up as 'an old guy thing.'" Today, Mike is sixty-four years old, and he finds himself doing 'the old guy thing' when addressing young women. "Mel is still rubbing off on me," Mike confesses.

Mike learned other things from Mel, like not backing down in the presence of error and getting out of your comfort zone. He also learned to trust God and the importance of prayer. God, through the love and discipleship of Mel and Tommy, took this tough kid who left Buckner Boys Home cussing the head woman, and turned him into a devoted follower of Christ. By the way, he now calls that head woman "Maw," and has ever since boot camp.

Margaret Ashmore

Sitting in Mel's living room with Mel by her side, Margaret begins her story. "I've often said if there were degrees of lostness, I was probably one of the most lost people you'd ever know. I wasn't raised in a Christian home, but I knew something was missing. I did what a lot of lost people do. I looked for it in the world—in drugs and wrong relationships. None of it ever satisfies. It only drives you deeper into loneliness and despair.

"I transferred from East Texas State University in Commerce to UNT, graduating in 1978. I was an artist and heard there were grants for artists. Here I am, just this lost person with a deep cavern of emptiness inside of me. Whenever you live that way, life never gets better; it just spirals downward, and that was the direction my life was going. I had a crush on a guy that was going to a Bible study Tommy was doing. I went because I thought this guy was cute. Tommy spoke on the last seven words of Christ and the six hours Christ hung on the cross. I remember Tommy saying, 'Jesus didn't die just for the world. He died for you.' He'd never set eyes on me, but he pointed right at me. At that moment, I knew there was something beyond myself."

After the meeting, Margaret asked Tommy if she could talk to him. She met with him the next morning, and he shared the gospel with her. Margaret can't point to the exact moment she received Christ, but life was starting to stir within her soul. As she met with Tommy at his house on Malone Street, he told her, "You need to go see a man named Mel Sumrall."

Margaret remembers, "Here I was, so hungry. I'd do whatever it took to satisfy this need in my heart. I showed up at Mel's doorstep. I walked through the door, and Mel sat me down in his living room. My first impression of Mel was that he was a man who loved with the love of Christ. Tommy shared the gospel with me; and that was the seed. Mel started watering it. That's what Mel does. Everywhere he goes, there's life. Mel tells me, 'Margaret, you need to get discipled.' Mel told her to go see a woman named Kay Bass (formerly Bodecher). Margaret said, "Because of Mel's heart, his care for me, and his desire that I grow in Christ; I made a beeline to Kay's house. She began to disciple me, and that was thirty-eight years ago."

Margaret got involved in missions. She explains, "I was good friends with a guy named James Skinner. Around 1990, Mel asked James to go to Nepal with him. I was asked to join them because I knew James. I'd hardly been out of Texas. I had never been on a mission trip. I knew one thing: I was going with Mel and Patty Lou. I knew they were going to guide me and teach me, so I went. I got to be with the master of the mission field," Margaret says. "Mel is a natural on the mission field. That's what God fashioned him to do. All Mel cares about is that men and women who have never heard the gospel, hear the Good News of Jesus Christ, are born again, and then discipled.

"I saw how Mel loved those people. He gave every one of them dignity. He was respectful to their culture. There was never a sense of 'I'm an American, and you're going to hear what I have to say.' He blended in and became all things to all men. I watched him show respect and honor. I love this about Mel, and I learned it from him. He won the opportunity to share Christ with them. He loved them in such a way that they wanted to hear what he believed. That was the beauty of Mel and Patty. They so loved people that people wanted to know what was in their hearts."

Margaret continues, "No matter how many obstacles Mel had, no matter how he felt, or how many aches and pains he had, he and Patty were faithful to get on a plane and go. Mel doesn't like to fly because of claustrophobia. He's a man who says, 'I don't like this, but for the glory of Christ, for the good of the kingdom of God, I'm going to get on this plane.' He was faithful and had courage to overcome his own fears for the sake of the gospel."

Mel recalls the first trip Margaret took with him and Patty. "We were going to Nepal, and we were waiting to meet Margaret in the Thailand airport. Her plane came in, and no Margaret. This was before cell phones, so we had no way to get in touch with her. We waited until two or three more flights came in. Still no Margaret. Finally, as we were leaving we ran into her in the baggage area. She was on the wrong floor!" Margaret says, "Here I am, this east Texas girl in Thailand. I am so lost. It's the grace of God that we ran into each other. Here they waited and waited, but they weren't upset. What did I get from them? Cheer and happiness and joy, and 'We're so glad to see you,' and some flowers. That was a remark-able moment."

On the way back home, Margaret had a harrowing experience in Bangkok, one of the biggest drug capitals in the world. Margaret says, "The police called me out of line at the airport and interrogated me. I'm this five feet, eleven inch single woman traveling alone, and I looked suspicious. Women over there travel with their husbands and are short. They put me in an interrogation room and asked me, 'Have you ever seen the inside of a Bangkok prison?' I said, 'No sir.' They tore into my luggage. Of course, there was nothing there; so, they let me go."

Margaret stayed with a woman named Manu Rongong in Nepal. Her husband spent six years in prison for sharing the gospel and leading someone to Christ. Margaret says, "Manu was an exceptional woman of God, sold out for Christ. You only meet a woman like her once in your lifetime. She would get on buses and go all over Nepal and India sharing the gospel."

One of Mel and Margaret's favorite stories is how Margaret got the nickname Sagarmatha. "Mel flew me to Siliguri, India to teach women there," Margaret remembers. "I flew over the Himalayas on a little plane with a goat on the plane, and we landed on a small dirt strip. The women in India are about five feet, and here I am five feet eleven. I get there, and some of the women in broken English start calling me a nickname. They said, 'Oh, it's Sagarmatha.' I remember thinking, 'Maybe it means brown-eyed woman or tall person.' The day before I flew back home, Mel and Patty and I took a rickshaw ride to a tourist shop in Kathmandu, Nepal. We walk into this tourist shop, and there's this big poster of Mount Everest. The Nepalese name for Mount Everest is Sagarmatha. All these women were calling me Mount Everest the whole time! Mel still calls me Sagarmatha sometimes."

When Margaret was saying goodbye to go to the airport, Manu said, "We all need to pray for Sagarmatha." Margaret thought, 'That's great. I need prayer.' But what Manu prayed surprised me. She laid hands on me and was lamenting the fact that I was leaving India where the gospel is flourishing and going back to America where everything is so easy. She felt sorry for *me* that I was going back to America! She was afraid for *me* spiritually because people in America are so spoiled. The message to the church of Laodicea in Revelation 3:17 states, 'You say, "I am rich, and have become wealthy, and have need of nothing," Here's this woman who had nothing. Most of the women at this conference lived in huts with dirt floors, and they were afraid for *me* because I was going back to the land of plenty."

Margaret remembers another time when she was in Africa. She was standing in this thatched area with open walls and teaching through a translator. She looked up and saw bats, but not regular bats. Vampire bats hung over her head. But Mel had taught her to press on. Margaret says, "You don't say, 'Oh my gosh, I'm scared. I'm not coming back.' You press on and teach with vampire bats hanging over your head. So what? And we did see fruit. Because over there, they're hungry. That's what Mel knows. People over there are hungry to hear the good news about Jesus. Jesus said the fields are white for harvest. Go tell them." Over the years, Margaret has been on two trips to Nepal. She's also been to Africa, Ireland, Israel, Bangkok, India, and Japan.

Asked how her life has changed since becoming a Christian, Margaret replies, "I never thought that I would know what it was to be free. The way I was raised, the pain of my own past, wounds and neglect, caused me to lock myself up in a little prison because the world was too scary. I thought I would be one of those people who would never get out of the prison of my own emotions and have the freedom to love. Before I became a Christian, I loved myself. I still struggle with that some. It was all about 'How do I save myself? How do I protect myself? I don't want to ever be hurt again, so I'm just going to spend my whole life loving myself, protecting myself.' Because of Tommy and Mel impacting my life, I have been set free from that prison of self. I discovered the power of the cross. If you die to yourself, you'll find your life, you'll discover life. I found out that you can spend your whole life trying to fix yourself, or you can die to yourself and receive Christ's life. The great secret of my Christian life is I quit going to years of counseling, which is just talking about myself and is a refined trick of Satan to get you to look at yourself. Counseling only helps if it leads people to the cross. I finally said 'OK, here I am a born-again Christian. I still have strongholds. I'm going to die to my past, I'm going to die to the demands of my flesh, I'm going to die to what I think I have a right to.'

"What I want to tell the world is that the cross can set us free. We discover resurrection power when we die. If I'm holding on to my life, if I'm trying to save my life, what I think I have a right to, what I think I'm entitled to, what I think people owe me, I can be as born-again as the day is long and never discover the power of Christ. We need to take our 'self' sins to the cross, quit thinking about ourselves, quit our pity-party, quit thinking about what is owed us, and we need to die. I love the fact that God gives us custom-made crosses that have our names on them. 'Margaret, you get on this cross, and you stay there until you have resurrection power, until I raise you.' That's a recent thing that God has asked me to do. I'm discovering that even in the worst of times, if we will die to ourselves, then we will receive that power from on high. It's not about counseling; it is about the cross."

Mel has died to self. Margaret says, "Mel has lived his life behind the scenes. Mel has been content to live in the shadow of the Almighty. That's where God has used him greatly. Mel has planted, and he's watered, but he's given all the glory to God. He never said, 'Look what I did.' There are people you meet in this world that are like comets. They flash at night and it's bright, and they're spectacular. And then there are North Stars. They're just always there, always faithful, always shining against the night. I always knew Mel was there for me. I knew I had a faithful friend; I knew I had a faithful man of God that I could always get godly counsel from. I love my earthly dad, but he was not a spiritual man. I never had spiritual counsel until I sat with Mel. I love Mel; he's the world to me. He means everything to me. He has forever changed my life."

Jim Hill

Jim Hill found out that going to seminary did not keep a person from having a drinking problem. He had been at Dallas Seminary for a couple of years when his drinking interrupted his life. He started out drinking on Fourth of July, Christmas, and other holidays; then it progressed to weekends and increased more and more during the week. Jim was attending seminary but getting less and less effective for Christ. He was working a part-time job at night and not getting a lot of sleep.

Jim's wife, Fairlyon, was attending a *Titus 2* study when Jim's drinking started. As it progressed, she finally spilled the beans to the women in her group. Jim and Fairlyon were in a *Colossians 2:7* group, and one night Mel and Patty attended. Jim was doing an internship under Mel, and when Mel found out about Jim's drinking problem, he told him, "Come on over. We need to talk about this."

Jim says, "I prayed with my wife before I went. I wanted to die on the way to meet Mel, but he was very loving and caring and gracious. He told me, 'I don't know if you're an alcoholic or not, but I don't have time to spend with you. You go to that counselor at the seminary. You've already paid for that in your tuition. Then get back to me.'" Jim wept and went for a couple of weeks without seeing the counselor. Mel asked him, "How are you doing with that drinking?" Jim told him, "I'm doing really great. I went two weeks, and then I drank a six-pack last night. Mel said, "Jim, you can't do that!"

It sounded perfectly normal to Jim; two whole weeks without a drink. But Mel once again told Jim, "You need to go to that counselor at DTS." Jim did. After four counseling sessions, he began rehab in Denton. Jim recalls, "Mel, the tough old crusty Marine leader, made me accountable, but he handled me with sensitivity. I started rehab on April 15, 1984, and I haven't had a drink since. I was in rehab 30 days. In the middle of that 30 days Mel got permission to visit me. 'How's it going? You doing OK?'" he asked Jim. Mel told him to hang in there, hang tough, do what you must do. That got him on the road to recovery. Mel has a gift of coming alongside hurting people and helping them get back on their feet. He doesn't give up on people.

Jim thought he would be going back to seminary in a few months, but he needed time to repair the damage he'd done with his wife and kids. Seven years passed before he went back to seminary. "I went to Bible studies as much as I could," Jim recalls. "One was at Mel's house with about thirty guys. Two or three of us were married, and the rest were single guys. It was a twelve-session, Christian-manhood type of thing. I availed myself of a lot of men's Bible studies just trying to grow spiritually."

Jim wondered what he should do since withdrawing from seminary. He told an old friend about his drinking problem. This friend had started a company, and he hired Jim as one of his first employees. One day, Mel asked Jim, "When are you going back to seminary and get your degree?" Jim replied, "Aw, they wouldn't take me back. I dropped courses and messed things up."

"Well, let's try," Mel responded. Jim talked to a woman in charge of admissions at DTS. She looked at Jim's records and said, "Man, this is going to take some time." The seminary had changed the degree requirements since Jim had attended seven years earlier. He had some good hours, and he had hours that he didn't need anymore. Jim had been pursuing a Master of Theology, but when he returned, he decided to get a two-year degree so at least he'd have something. He ended up with ninety hours for a degree that only required sixty hours. Someone told him, "Boy, Jim, that's a really beefed up Master of Biblical Studies program you completed." Jim eventually took the other thirty hours and got his Th.M. in 1993.

When Denton Bible was getting ready to build their second building, The Mill, in 1991, they realized they needed someone with an accounting background. Tommy called Jim and asked him if he was interested in coming on staff. Jim was hired several months later and remained on staff until he retired in 2017. Jim says, "When I came on staff, Mel and Tommy knew all my struggles, all of my warts, all of my difficulties. Mel would say, 'You know, a lot of churches shoot their wounded. We're like a hospital rehab. We want to help you recover and be effective for the Lord.' I've used it in our Christian AA group."

Jim says of Mel, "He was a visionary. He would look at these new ideas and things to do, and then he would challenge the leadership. Jim traveled to Mongolia with Mel and Patty in the 1990s. "There were about fifty believers in the whole country of seven or eight million people," Jim says. "Toward the end, after they got transportation going, there were ten thousand believers. It started out very small, but look what God did!"

Reflecting on Mel's impact on his life personally, Jim comments, "I look at Mel as giving balance to the Christian walk. If it hadn't been for Mel appealing to me when I had the alcohol problem, I hate to think where Fairlyon and I would be without him and Denton Bible Church leadership during that time of our lives. God led us to Dallas so I could go to seminary. God led us to Denton Bible to grow and serve Him. Mel, of course, was a major part of that.

"When I was about a year sober, Mel said, 'I want you to teach this adult Sunday school class.' I said, 'Oh, Mel, I don't feel worthy of doing that.' He replied, 'Dad gum it, Jim, if we all waited until we felt worthy enough to serve the Lord, nothing would ever get done for the kingdom of God!' I taught the Sunday school class." Jim says, "Mel constantly pushes people out of their comfort zone. He can do that, because he himself continually walks by faith, obeying God even when it's inconvenient, uncomfortable, or downright scary. May God raise up men and women who follow Mel's example and dare great things for God."

Many times, it was inconvenient, uncomfortable, or downright scary for Mel and Patty as they traveled the world serving God. However, their faith never faltered as they trusted God in dangerous situations.

Chapter 16

Stories from the Mission Field

As Mel and Patty served the Lord around the world, they never knew what they would face when they got on a plane. Once they were taking off from Bangkok, Thailand to fly to Bangladesh. The plane was at the end of the runway. Mel says, "I could see the white stripes on the runway. The plane was at full throttle taking off, and suddenly, the plane began to veer off the white lines. People were screaming, the brakes were squealing, and the pilot was trying to get control of the plane. It finally stopped with two wheels off the runway and in the field. That was bad enough," Mel says. "But the Thai pilot got the plane back on the taxi strip, and in his broken English he said, 'I think my brakes locked. We'll try again.' They were going down the runway again at full throttle again, and the plane goes out in the field. Here came the fire trucks and the emergency vehicles. Mel and Patty were thinking, "We're going to be burned alive." Thankfully the plane didn't catch fire, and Mel and Patty made it safely off.

Another time, they were in one of the larger planes flying from Japan to Thailand. As they cruised at thirty-nine thousand feet something grabbed the plane. Mel says, "I've never been in that kind of vibration in my life. People screamed, fear written all over their faces. Patty was in the seat next to me." When Mel looked out the window, he saw the wings flopping up and down. Mel grabbed Patty, held her tight, and said, "This is the end, Sweetheart." However, after a few minutes, the phenomenon ended. Mel never learned what caused the problem. "There was a typhoon in the area," he says. "I don't know if the vibration came from the wash of that or the jet stream." Yet again, they could have died.

Mel recalls another instance involving Daniel Lamb, a Chinese businessman. The Lord dramatically changed his life, and he sold his businesses and used the money to start Bible colleges in Asia. God brought Mel and Daniel together, and they started doing ministry in places like Siberia. Mel and Patty were in Bangalore, India, teaching *BTCP*. Mel got a call from Daniel who was in Omsk, Russia where he was scheduled for a planning session in a couple of weeks. Mel explains, "Daniel wanted to know if Patty and I could attend, as well. I told him we'd come. After the meeting in Russia, Daniel would accompany Patty and me to Mongolia. Daniel told me, 'I'll get the tickets for you to fly from Moscow to Hong Kong on a Russian jet. Then we'll fly from Hong Kong to Beijing and pick up our papers to go to Mongolia.' I told him, "That sounds fine.'"

Two weeks later, Mel and Patty were sick with diarrhea caused by the food or the water. Mel called Daniel and told him that he and Patty couldn't make it; they needed to head back to the U.S. and recuperate. Daniel decided to continue with the agenda without the Sumralls. Mel was sitting on the couch in his Texas home watching the news, and a story aired about a Russian jet flying from Mongolia to Hong Kong that crashed, killing everybody aboard. Daniel Lamb died on that plane along with everyone else. Mel adds, "That's the plane we were supposed to be on."

Another narrow escape with death occurred when Mel and Patty taught for a semester at the International School of Theology in the Philippines. Remembering his time as a Marine during World War II, Mel states, "The Japanese had conquered the Philippine islands, and they were going to use it for attacks on places like Australia and New Zealand. The U.S. had to take the Philippine islands back from the Japanese. When General MacArthur, the five-star Supreme Commander, went to the Philippines, he took a detachment of Marines with him. I was one of those Marines." Having been injured by shrapnel, Mel could've received a Purple Heart, but he never reported it.

The American bases at Subic Field and Clark Field in the Philippines were due for renewal in the 1990s when Mel and Patty were teaching at the theological school. About eighty thousand American troops were stationed there at that time. Some Philippine citizens opposed the Americans staying in the Philippines, and then Communists became involved. To discourage the Americans from staying in the Philippines, they formed hit teams and killed nine Americans while Mel and Patty were there.

One morning, Mel and Patty stepped out of the house where they were staying. They headed across a field to get a ride from a South Korean student. Mel noticed a guy standing in the fields. Mel wondered, "What is that guy doing standing there? He can't get a ride from there. He's just standing in the field." Mel and Patty would have to go past this guy to catch their ride. Then Mel saw another man coming along a fence on the other side of the field. Mel and Patty were sandwiched between them.

"And here came the assassin," Mel says. "He had on tennis shoes and a blue jacket with his right hand in his pocket. He came right at us. He was just a few feet away. The hit men were using 45 pistols which are lethal weapons but are difficult to get a good aim."

Mel yelled to him, "Good morning, son, how are you?" The man stopped, turned his head to the side and went several paces to the right. Having been in the Marines during World War II and the Korean War, Mel had seen men with terror on their faces. But he'd never seen anyone as terrified as this man.

The man started toward Mel and Patty again. He took three or four paces, and Mel yelled again, "Good morning, son, how are you?" The man backed off.

Mel asked Patty, "Did you see what just happened?"

She responded, "No, I was watching my shoes and trying not to step in the open sewage running down the street."

When Mel got to the seminary, he visited the academic dean to tell him what had happened. The dean called the American Embassy, and the American Embassy called the police. The police said, "Send the Americans to the jail." The police had caught some men who might be Communist hit men and wanted Mel and Patty to identify them. Mel and Patty went to the police department and spent two

143

hours trying to identify the men. Mel concludes, "It was a harrowing experience."

Mel and Patty learned that nothing happens to us until God is ready to take us to heaven. Mel says, "We all know that in our head, but when you live through life-threatening experiences like Patty and I did, you really believe it. We need to be in much prayer for our missionaries because it's not all hip-hip-hurray."

In addition to dangerous situations, Mel and Patty had some fascinating experiences. Mel helped start *Bible Training Center for Pastors* in Ecuador through a contact named Freddy Guerro. In Ecuador, five missionaries, including Jim Elliot, were martyred in the 1950s. The Auca Indians, who killed the missionaries, lived near another group of native peoples called the Quichua. The Lord brought a revival to the Quichua Indians, and that's who Mel and others were training in *BTCP*. When the first class graduated, Mel and Patty were invited to attend. Quito, the capital of Ecuador, is at nine thousand feet elevation. Mel recalls, "Active volcanos are all over the place with flights sometimes cancelled because the ash might get in the engines of the planes." When they went to the *BTCP* graduation, they landed at Quito and then flew to Riobamba where the graduation would be held. "There were no commercial flights to Riobamba," Mel says, "so a Missionary Aviation Pilot was scheduled to fly us there. We waited and waited, wondering where the plane was. It finally landed, and a female missionary was carried off. She'd been attacked by a wild pig and was bleeding profusely from her arms and legs. The hospital ambulance carried her off."

The pilot, Henry, was completing his log, and Mel asked him, "Henry, do you know anything about Palm Beach?" Palm Beach was the code name used by the five missionaries who were killed trying to reach the Auca Indians. Henry said he did. Mel asked, "Could you take us to where it happened?"

Henry flew them to the area and then said, "Pastor Mel, I'd like you to get a feel for what it's like to land on a sandbar in the river. That's what the five missionaries did to reach the Auca Indians." Mel asked Henry, "How many hours do you have in this plane?"

"About ten thousand."

"Well, OK," Mel responded.

Henry turned the plane until it was going sideways up the river with trees on both sides. Finally, down they went. Then Henry asked Mel and Patty, "Would you like to see where Elizabeth Elliott and Rachel Saint lived when their loved ones were killed?" Henry flew them over the former dwelling place. Afterwards, Henry flew them to Riobamba. "It was a marvelous thing," Mel says. "The Quichua built this church which was rustic, but they did the best they could." Lining the walkway into the church were people in white ponchos on one side and red ponchos on the other side. Mel and Patty went inside. They saw people weeping and crying, because they never expected to receive a Biblical education like *BTCP*. The next day, Mel got a call from the radio station in Riobamba which aired HCJB. They wanted Mel to speak. The program aired all over South America and led to openings for teaching *BTCP* in Argentina, Brazil, Columbia, Chile and many other countries.

One evening in Riobamba, Mel and Patty had dinner in Ecuador's version of a banquet hall. They sat up front, and the nearest table was about ten feet away from them. The meal arrived, and it was an animal like a rat. Mel was uncertain if it was a rat, but he stared at this creature all stretched out in the dish. A guy at the end of the table said, "Pastor, you're not eating your food." It was about nine o'clock at night, so Mel told him, "I can't eat food this late at night." Remembering the experience, Mel exclaims, "I couldn't eat that critter!" But Mel also recalls the time he and Patty had the opportunity to eat grasshoppers in Alexandria, Egypt, "We got those down."

Mel and Patty flew back to Quito to leave Ecuador and return to Orlando, Florida, where flights to and from Quito originate. Mel and Patty got on the plane and began talking about the book Elizabeth Elliot wrote, *Through Gates of Splendor*, chronicling the death of her husband Jim and the four other missionaries. The man sitting in from of them turned and asked them, "How do you folks know about *Gates of Splendor*?"

When Mel told him, the guy stuck out his right hand and said, "I always wear my father's wedding ring. That way I know my father is always with me."

"Which one of the five missionaries was your father?" Mel asked.

"Roger Youderian," he responded. Mel spent about two hours on the flight from Quito to Orlando talking to Jerome Youderian. He told Mel stories that many people had never heard.

Mel remembered when the five missionaries were killed in the '50s. Even though he was far from the Lord at the time, he thought, "I wonder if the Lord would want me to replace one of those missionaries?" Mel may not have replaced one of the five missionaries, but God definitely called him to missions. Mel had a sensitive heart to circumstances surrounding him on the mission field. Once in Bangladesh, Mel asked the men to open their Bibles to a certain passage. As he opened his Bible, he didn't hear any ruffling of pages. Mel realized that of the two hundred men attending the leadership conference, only a few had a Bible. Bangladesh is about ninety nine percent Muslim, and Christians are very poor.

Mel asked one of the men in charge, "Is there a bookstore in town that would have Bibles in your language?" The man answered affirmatively. Mel shut down the conference, bought all the Bibles available, and handed them out to the men. After the conference, Mel and Patty prepared to head home when a monsoon struck. Bangladesh is a very flat country where the rain doesn't come straight down; it rains horizontally. Mel watched the men from the conference as they left. "They had these flimsy raincoats which probably cost fifty cents, but they hit that monsoon rain bare-skinned because they wrapped their raincoats around their Bibles."

Another time Mel visited a village in Bangladesh. The road leading to the village had no pavement, only dirt. When Mel got to the village, he was directed to a place of honor. "There was a guy on each side fanning me," Mel laughs. "Like I was King Bubba."

Although Mel primarily taught *BTCP*, he didn't hesitate when he needed to utilize other resources on the mission field. When he taught in Venezuela, he discovered that some of the worst prisons in the world existed there. Mel had materials from the jail ministry at Denton Bible Church translated into Spanish, and he sent a couple to Venezuela to train people how to do jail ministry. The last Mel heard, this couple went to South Texas to learn Spanish to prepare for full-time jail ministry in Venezuela. Divorce is a big problem in Venezuela, even among pastors. Mel had the materials used at

Denton Bible Church for pre-marital counseling translated into Spanish. Then, he sent a DBC elder, Dick Craven, and his wife, Gini, to train people in Venezuela. Mel comments, "They were about five feet off the ground when they got back."

In the late '90s, Patty and Mel went to Dhaka, the capital of Bangladesh, to start *BTCP*. Accompanied by one of his disciples, they came through Calcutta on their way home. The young man asked, "Pastor Mel, would you and Patty like to meet Mother Teresa?"

"Oh, my, yes, that would be a great honor," Mel responded.

The young man knew her, so he called and made an appointment. "I was amazed at how tiny she was, less than five feet tall," Mel says. "My Patty was five feet and two inches tall, Mother Teresa looked so short compared to Patty. She spoke good English. We got to visit with her for about half an hour. One thing that struck me was that she didn't have any shoes on. Her feet were badly deformed. I remember Patty saying, 'Mother Teresa, I'm sorry about your feet.' Mother Teresa replied, 'It's OK, we don't pay any attention to that kind of thing.'"

Mother Teresa showed Mel and Patty around her ministry. Several of the females were working. All kinds of pictures hung on the walls. Mel says, "I realized how the Catholic religion thinks they're going to work their way to heaven. From our side of the fence, we sometimes think that's a great barrier; they won't make it. As I looked at her and heard her stories, I couldn't imagine that she wouldn't be in heaven despite her theology. I remembered that verse, "Believe on the Lord Jesus Christ, and thou shalt be saved' (Acts 16:31)."

Mel remembers, "She showed such love for the Lord. She and her staff would go around Calcutta when she was alive, and they would pick up little babies and orphans and take them in. I remember she stayed with one man until he passed away. He was laying out on the street, and rats had been gnawing on his body. He couldn't do anything to help himself. She stayed with him and tried to comfort him until he died."

Mel's stories from the mission field help him illustrate God's faithfulness to the men he disciples. Mel grows their faith by spending time with them. He loves these men, and they know it. He stands by them in the ups and downs of their lives. In turn, the men stand by Mel in their love and devotion to him.

Chapter 17

What Discipleship Looks Like

W hen Bryan Collins and his wife Lori pulled into the parking lot of Denton Bible Church in 1988, they had no idea this would be a life-changing event for them. They were running late, and the parking lot was full. Denton Bible was meeting at the time in what is now the Sumrall Center.

Bryan says, "Standing at the edge of the parking lot was this old guy, and he was the first one to greet us. It was Mel, and he was very friendly. Later we found out that he was the senior pastor. It made quite an impression on us that he would be greeting people, especially the latecomers."

Lori and Bryan were there when Mel began taking *BTCP* to various places around the world. Bryan heard that Mel needed someone to mow his yard. He thought, "If Mel can go all over the world, I can certainly mow his yard." Bryan mowed Mel's yard every week. "Mel would come out and chat a little bit, and he was very appreciative. I got to know him that way. I was at his house mowing one day, and Mel asked me what I was going to be doing in five years. I found out later that Mel constantly challenges people."

Bryan and his wife were part of a *2:7* group led by John Bordeaux. When John planted a church from DBC in 1990, Denton Community Church, Bryan was part of the team. Mel challenged Bryan to go to seminary, and he graduated from DTS in 1996 with a Master of Biblical Studies. John Bordeaux eventually left Denton Community Church, and Wayne Stiles took over as senior pastor with Bryan as the associate pastor. Stiles left in 2005, and Bryan stepped in as senior pastor where he continues to serve in that position.

Bryan has watched Mel lead by example when he faced huge obstacles. "Mel, as much as he travels all over the world, has serious claustrophobia," Bryan says. "James Arnold, when he was working with Mel and making travel arrangements, would try to get him the same seats on the plane. Patty would have to calm him. Even with that obstacle, Mel was flying all over the place. Every one of those plane trips was a challenge for him. When my wife was diagnosed with cancer, we were at the hospital on the fourth floor. At that time, he was having a real battle with the claustrophobia. He could hardly be in a restaurant because it felt like things were closing in. I was in the room with Lori, and Mel came walking in. I knew the only way he could have gotten there was to get in an elevator. He did it for her."

Sadly, Lori passed away in 2012. Bryan continued raising his daughters, Kaycee and Allyson. Kaycee is now twenty three and works as a firefighter with Farmers Branch. Allyson is nineteen and getting her EMT at North Central Texas College. Understandably, Bryan is very proud of them. He remembers taking Kaycee to Mel's house when she was about two or three years old. Mel's mom was living with Mel and Patty at the time, and she was about a hundred years old. "She would take Kaycee on her knee and let her ride the horse." Bryan says. "Amazing!"

Mel has always been there to encourage Bryan. They started meeting for lunch every week in 2000 and still do. There was never any formal discipleship, but Bryan has learned much from Mel just being around him. Whether it was meeting for catfish or Cajun food, or helping Mel around the house, Bryan had the opportunity to talk about everything from pastoring to enduring life's hardships. Bryan comments, "I've learned more about pastoring from being around Mel and watching him than I ever did in seminary. Mel is solid in the Scriptures, and he loves people. One of the greatest lessons I've learned from him is to love the people in front of you. God has blessed Mel with a long ministry. He's gone all over the world, and he remembers individuals and their stories. He knows what being a good shepherd is and fulfills it well." Mel is a father figure to Bryan.

"He's always been very caring and loving. Much of my life and the direction it's taken has been because of Mel's leading and prodding and guidance."

Bryan's final thoughts about Mel: "He will always find some way to be useful. He's always dreaming. I was meeting a guy for lunch at Cracker Barrel, and Mel came in and was talking with another guy. I went over to say hello and asked him what they were talking about. Mel said, 'We were talking about how to save Nepal.' He's always thought in giant terms. That's the way Mel thinks. I was just trying to figure out if I was going to have pancakes or not."

Mel has spent years pouring into John Brown as well. He and John began their weekly meetings in 2007. John says of Mel, "He is my friend, model, and discipler. He has been a constant encouragement and blessing to me. He reminds me that—for all the sin in the world and in the church—great saints of God *do* still walk the earth."

John was born in Lubbock, raised in Denton, and graduated from the University of Texas in Austin. He came to Christ through a "Tommy tape" the summer after his sophomore year of college. After graduating from college, he attended Tommy's Young Guns discipleship program for men at Denton Bible Church in 1992-1993. He worked briefly at the Probe Center in Austin, then entered Dallas Theological Seminary in 1994. John graduated in 2000 with a Master of Arts in Biblical Studies, Master of Theology, and completed a year of the doctoral program.

Around 2000, James Arnold—missions pastor at Denton Bible Church—contacted John about writing a book on church history for use in training pastors overseas. As a result, John began as an intern at the DBC missions office and helped develop and implement the Missionary Training Institute which is still in effect. In January 2001 he joined the DBC staff. In 2008 he wrote the *Man of God* study which is the counterpart to *The Titus 2 Woman*. It has been translated into Spanish, French, Romanian, Chinese and Russian and is still in use today in missions and with the men's ministry at DBC. John worked with the missions department until 2014. Since that time John has worked with Be United in Christ Outreach Ministry.

John met Mel after he joined the staff of the SERVE missions department. Although he never traveled with Mel on mission trips, he did have the opportunity to go with Mel and Alan Chamberlain to Pueblo, Colorado, to meet Mel's discipler, Ron Chadwick, after Ron had a stroke in 2015. It touched Mel's heart when John and Alan told Mel, "We're flying with you to see Ron." Several things stand out to John about that trip.

"I was impressed by how large CF&I (Mel's former employer) was, and the level of responsibility Mel had," John said. "Then I was amazed to learn that Mel had built his home and dug the well there himself." It touched John to visit the grave sites of Mel's parents, sister, and baby daughter. John realized how much Mel gave up when he moved to Texas in answering God's call to ministry.

In the following list, John shares a few of the many lessons he has learned from Mel:

a. Mel once said, "Pastors need thick skins and soft hearts, but many have thin skins and hard hearts." Mel lives out the former.

b. Mel is the paradigm of faithfulness and unceasing service for his Lord. He is always thinking about new ways to reach new groups and do more for Christ. He will die in harness straining forward, which is a great inspiration to all of us.

c. Mel was a model husband who taught us what it looks like to love and serve our wives faithfully to the very end.

d. Mel has suffered much and forgiven much.

e. Mel is a compassionate man. I have heard him many times pray under his breath, "Lord, help that person; their life must be so hard."

f. Mel is a kind man, initiating contact with strangers and encouraging everyone he meets.

g. For everyone privileged to know him, Mel is who we want to be when we grow up.

Mel ends his phone calls with John by saying, "I love you, son." This touches John every time. He says, "I love Mel, and I'm privileged and blessed to have him in my life."

Alan Chamberlain was also touched by the visit to Pueblo when he and John Brown took Mel to visit Ron Chadwick. Alan says, "That trip was profound. That is the headwaters for Mel and for Denton Bible Church. That town created Mel, from his humble beginnings to his success as a businessman."

Alan reflects on visiting the graves of Mel's father and baby daughter, Pamela, "I stood at his dad's grave and saw this older man become a child again as he thought about being sixteen years old and his dad dying. Then we visited Pamela's grave, and your mind goes back to Mel as a young married man losing his baby. That was part of what made Mel, what drove him deeper to Christ and deeper into what became his life's work. To stand at the grave of his daughter and think, 'Who could have predicted the impact this would have on tens of thousands of people around the world' was significant for me."

Mel's influence is global but also personal. Alan and his wife Linda have been members of Denton Bible Church since 2000. Alan served as an elder from 2008 until 2012. Alan says, "Elders oversee different ministries and different folks, and I asked for Mel. We always hit it off. He had a business background, and he fascinated me because he went from the military to the business world to the pastorate, and I grew up in a pastor's home. It's been my desire to get out of business and go into ministry. Mel did that successfully late in life. One of my questions then and now is 'How can we marry these two?' Mel was always wise and knowledgeable and had been down the path. From a leadership perspective, a practical perspective, and a ministerial perspective—he pulled it all together."

Alan's life verse is Matthew 6:33: "But seek first His kingdom and His righteousness, and all these things will be given to you as well." He comments, "I can get caught up in the temporal, the material, just stuff and silliness and the tyranny of the urgent. Mel at ninety-two keeps striving towards what's important. It's people, it's ministry, it's the kingdom, what God is doing. You can't be around Mel long before the conversation turns to that. I always leave Mel thinking, 'I want that to be my focus when I'm ninety-two.' Mel is the standard."

Alan says, "When Mel meets someone, he asks, 'How are you,' and then 'How's your spiritual life?' There's an old Scottish proverb, 'No one should be allowed to play the violin until they have mastered it.' That's not Mel's position. Mel says, 'We've got to get you out there. We've got to get you on a plane.' He continues to push people out of their comfort zone. If you fail, he doesn't beat you down; he builds you up."

To Alan, Mel is a dear friend, a dear mentor, and the true definition of a pastor. "He's an example of what we need to be as we get older," Alan says. "Still leading, still serving, still concerned about the kingdom of God."

Cary Hull, another young man whom Mel took under his wing, moved to Denton eleven years ago. As a single man in his thirties, he looked for a church and found Denton Bible where Tommy was preaching through Romans. "He was in Romans 1:1. I had never heard expository preaching the way Tommy preaches it," Cary says. "He walks us through the Bible, verse by verse."

Although Cary "hid out" for about a year, he eventually got to know people and began serving. "I think I hid out because of my immaturity," Cary relates. "God has used DBC to grow my faith, mature me, and to teach me a lot about myself and the Lord." In addition to Tommy's preaching, God grew Cary in a huge way through his time with Mel. He remembers how Mel came into his life. "There was a girl in the women's discipleship program at DBC," Cary says. "She and I wanted to date, but we couldn't because of her being in the women's program. It's a very intense nine-month program, and the women commit to no dating during that time."

One day this girl told Cary, "There's this man who meets with young men at his home and disciples them." She gave Cary Mel's name and address. It turned out that this girl lived with Mel and Patty, just one of seventy-eight girls who lived with them over a thirty-five-year period. Cary called Mel, and he said, "Yes, son, come join our group tonight." The group was meeting for dinner at the Trail Dust Steakhouse. Cary got there and saw this older man with all these guys in their twenties. They welcomed him into the group, and the following week Cary met at Mel's house with the guys and began a long, loving relationship with Mel. That was in

2006, and that relationship continues to this day. Cary stayed in the group for about four years, even though others would leave and new guys would join.

Through this time, Cary saw Mel's heart for discipleship. "If you go to Mel's house, you'll see all these legal pads with notes and programs for discipling people. Over the years, he's seen what works and what doesn't work. He's constantly thinking through different ways of presenting truth so it's more palatable. To see young men come in, be teachable, and grow is a joy for Mel. He faithfully meets with them, but he also prays for them during the week." Cary says, "Mel loves discipleship, but it's not just discipleship. He loves young men and women."

Cary met with Mel for about a year when Mel told the story of how *BTCP* got started. Cary asked him, "What is this *BTCP*?" Mel shared the vision God gave him twenty years ago of the need to train pastors and leaders in churches. Cary wept when he heard it. "I had never thought of that," Cary says. "God had already accomplished much of that vision through our church and our SERVE missions department using *BTCP* around the world. I wanted to be part of it. Mel encouraged me to go through *BTCP*. I got some friends together and we went through it. It's one of the best programs I've been through. It sets you up for ministry and to serve effectively. About halfway through, I started teaching at a nursing home, and I'd never done anything like that in my life. A couple of summers ago, I went to China to teach pastors, and I never thought I would do that. I trace all this back to the conversation I had with Mel in his home about *BTCP*," Cary says.

Cary saw a gradual transition during the time that Mel was discipling him. "Miss Patty started to decline," Cary says. "It was hard for Mel during this time. He had to shift his role from being an amazing discipler who spent a lot of time serving the Lord, to serving his wife more and more. It wasn't easy, but he did it because of his love and commitment to his sweetheart. To see him day in and day out not going to events that he would love to go to was a great example to me. He would say, "I'm staying here with my wife." To see him love *people* well is one thing, but to see him love his *wife* well was beautiful."

Mel would tell the young guys he was discipling, "You need to find you a good Christian woman and marry her. Make some babies and bring them around." Cary met Meredith, his future wife; they were friends for a year before they started dating. "When we started dating, I knew I wanted to marry her," Cary says. I asked Mel, 'Should it be a long engagement?' He said, "No. Not a long engagement. Do it quickly.'"

Cary and Meredith were engaged for ten weeks. There wasn't enough time for the church to do the premarital counseling, so Mel offered to do it. He married them on December 11, 2010. Cary says, "After the wedding, you're supposed to turn around and face every-body, and then go back down the aisle. We just took off running. When it was Mel's turn to walk down, he took off running too. We had people coming up to us saying, 'That Pastor Mel, he's older, but he sure can run!'"

Cary and Meredith now have three children, ages three, two and nine months. "After our first child was born, it was a big deal to introduce him to Papa Mel. My whole family calls him Papa Mel. I cannot drive by his house without them yelling, 'Papa Mel's house; we've got to stop.' He loves the little children so well." Cary and Meredith named their last child Judah Melvin Luther Hull. Mel calls him Little Mel. One of Mel's favorite phrases when he gets frustrated is, 'Dad gum it.' Cary says, "I heard my three-year-old the other day say, 'Dad gum it.' Mel has made a big impression on him. I told Mel he has to stay around another twenty years so my boys can get to know him."

The Lord had been drawing Cary to ministry with international students. Around 2012 he had the opportunity to begin working with WorldLife, an outreach to international students at UNT. "When a big decision like that comes up, I run to Papa Mel and ask his advice. He's always been consistent with good advice." Cary joined WorldLife, and Mel would come with Patty to the dinners for inter-national students on Fridays at UNT. "He came because he loves international students. It was so nice having him there. We would sit Miss Patty in the chair, and Mel would visit with people. He did this until she wasn't able to come. It was encouraging that he would make time when it wasn't easy for him."

About five years ago, Cary was talking to Mel about discipleship, and he told Mel about a former pastor in Houston who was struggling. "He's a good guy, Mel, a Baptist preacher. I asked him about discipleship, and he had never heard of it." Mel said, 'Well, let's go see him.' The next thing I know we're in my truck heading south, driving four hours to get there. When we got there, Mel didn't blast him with knowledge. He loved on him and asked questions. We talked about discipleship some and his struggles. Then, we turned around and drove four hours back home. I don't know anybody in my life that would have done that with me, especially somebody of Mel's caliber. That's what's amazing about him. Mel Sumrall is the founder of our church, he's the pastor emeritus, and he's at a high caliber, but you wouldn't think that if you went and sat down with him. He'll talk to anybody, make time for anyone."

Cary says, "I've never met anyone who loves as well as Mel does. He loves people! A lot of times when you get close to a person, you can see their cracks and flaws. I've gotten close to Mel over the years. He's not perfect, but he's an amazing man. God has matured him in a way where he loves people well." Mel's endurance amazes Cary. "I go over there sometimes, and I'm exhausted after thirty minutes. I'm half his age. His mind is amazing. It's always working towards how to help people, how to bless people, how to glorify God. He's a visionary. Out of the overflow of the heart the mouth speaks, and he's always pushing other people. A lot of people don't have the vision or the energy for the calling that he does. Mel's endurance is incredible! I see how hard he's running. He's like a sprinter that's been running for thirty years."

Cary saw another example of Mel's endurance and ability to overcome obstacles in his life when Mel's sister was nearing the end of her life. He told Cary he had shared the gospel with her over and over, and she didn't respond. Mel said, "I'd love to share the gospel with her one more time." Cary said, "Next thing I know we're on an airplane going to Colorado to see his sister. The big challenge was that he hadn't flown in months. He had gradually gotten off his medication for claustrophobia, but he was still struggling with it. He had Scriptures to rest on, and I was reading him those Scriptures when we got on the plane. I watched him surrender to God and go to Colorado. He was obedient to the point of suffering. We flew to Denver, rented a car and drove to Greeley where his sister lived. We met with her, Mel shared the gospel, and she prayed to receive Christ at almost ninety years old. Mel was so happy about that. She passed away not too long after that."

Cary thinks about his personal life, spiritual life, and the ministry God has him plugged into. Cary says, "There's always a man I can look at, and he's doing it, he's been doing it for a long time. He's always been that man that I can go to and ask a question about something I'm struggling with theologically or personally or spiritually. He always has a biblical answer. He might give his opinion, but primarily he's going to tell me what God says. He's just so knowledgeable. How many people would listen to Mel if he just had a lot of knowledge? He's knowledgeable, but he's putting it into action, and he's been putting it into action for a long time. Mel is like my spiritual daddy; I've grown so much under him!"

Chapter 18

Mel the Overcomer

God used eighty-four-year-old Mel to plant a church. On December 21, 2009, Mel and Patty met with J. R. and Eve Roberts about starting a church in Decatur, Texas. Mel had stepped down from the staff of Denton Bible Church nine years earlier, but for Mel, there's no retirement for Christians. Despite health issues that go along with growing older, Mel continued to step out in faith.

Decatur Bible Church was birthed after years of prayer for a Bible church in Wise County. J. R. and Eve first heard about Tommy and Denton Bible while attending Prestonwood Baptist Church in 1992 where Tommy taught a Bible study for singles. From 1992 to 1998 J. R. and Eve listened to Tommy on cassette tapes and attended Denton Bible occasionally. In September 1998, they began attending Denton Bible full-time, commuting from Decatur which is about thirty miles from Denton.

Eve says, "We were sad that Denton Bible was so far away. It's hard to get plugged into a church when it's not in your hometown. However, we were so hungry for expository teaching from God's Word that we did it anyway. J. R. started praying fervently for a Bible church in Wise County." J. R. was transferred to Bolivia in 2001, and they lived there until 2003. Before they left for Bolivia, they went to the media ministry at DBC and got all the series that Tommy had taught. They became the Denton Bible Church and Tommy Nelson Lending Library in Bolivia. Only *Genesis* and *Romans* were on video; the other series were cassette tapes. When the Roberts moved back to America, they left the lending library with a missionary family.

After moving back to Decatur in 2003, J. R. and Eve worshipped with his aging parents in Decatur until they passed away. They continued to pray for a Bible church. In June 2009, they visited Sanger Bible Church, another Denton Bible church plant where John Brown was preaching. They talked to him after church, and he said, "Get your twelve and start praying." They did. From June through October, they watched Tommy's video sermons on Sunday nights in various homes around Decatur.

In November, the Roberts talked to Mike Scheer, missions pastor at Denton Bible Church, and a couple of elders. Ten days later, they met with Tommy and all the elders at DBC. Then one fateful day in November, J. R. and Eve got a voicemail from Mel. He said, "Tommy wants me to help y'all start a church." They saved that voicemail for a long time until the answering machine finally went away. J. R. and Eve had gotten to know Mel and Patty when Eve did a video of Mel's mom in honor of her hundredth birthday.

Mel and Patty met with J. R. and Eve at a restaurant in Denton on December 21, 2009 to discuss starting a church in Decatur. They had their twelve, and Mel said he would come over and take them through *2:7*. Mel and Patty began driving to Decatur in February 2010 every Wednesday. On April 25, 2010, Decatur Bible Church had its first Sunday morning service in the home of one of the twelve. DBC elder Jim Roberts and his wife Joan came for the inaugural service.

In 2011 Mel told them, "You need to have elders." Men were chosen and ordained. Mel still came on Wednesdays, but not to preaching on Sundays. Several different song leaders came from Denton Bible Church to lead worship on Sundays. Mel and Patty faithfully came, even though Patty's health was declining. Eve remembers Patty sitting in their living room with her eyes closed. "It was so sweet," Eve says, "Mel would touch her on the arm and ask her, 'Honey, was that such and such a date?' as he talked about mission trips they had taken. And she would say, 'No, it was on this date.' She was in and out but so present. She was adorable. Mel was always gentle and loving with her. She was his sweetheart."

Mel took the small congregation through two of the three 2:7 books before he and Patty stopped coming due to Patty's health. On July 4, 2011 Mel handed off the responsibility of Decatur Bible Church to someone else. Paul Polk, Aaron Campbell and Jody LeBlanc from Denton Bible Church rotated the preaching duties in 2012 and met with the elders at Decatur Bible Church to solidify its doctrinal foundation and formulate a procedure for securing its first pastor. On September 13, 2013, Rick Carman became the pastor and continues today. The church met in several different locations before buying a building at 700 N. Trinity in Decatur.

Eve says, "We learned from Mel not to let the teaching get in the way of relationships. You want to preach God's Word, but you can get so much about teaching that you forget the people and relationships. Mel gave us a list of thirty-five 'one anothers' (love one another, encourage one another, etc.) in the Bible, and I carry it with me.

"No matter how many days or months we're apart from each other, Mel treats me as if I'm the most special person in the world," Eve says. "That's an incredible blessing to me. It tells me that I'm special, and I need to do that to others. He knows me as a sister. Who on earth would you rather have as a brother in Christ than Mel Sumrall? To be able to say to my grave that Mel Sumrall knew me is huge. Jesus calls us by name, and He knows us. That's Mel."

Though Mel has been used greatly by God, like all believers, Mel has faced struggles through the years as the Lord stretched his faith. Asked if he has ever had doubts, Mel replies, "Oh, yes! We tend to think that because we have such a loving God that our life is going to be easy, that everything is going to fall into place. That's what we pray for. We ask, 'Why do I have to go through this suffering?'"

Mel and Patty were married almost seventy-one years when Patty passed away on June 26, 2017. The years and months preceding her death brought times of great suffering for Mel. One night he prayed, "Lord, what do You want to teach me with my wife laying here dying for so long? I love her so much, and I don't know what I'm going to do without her. She's been my strong right arm all these years, the most perfect wife a man could have. I've been so blessed by her."

He had questions and doubts about what it was going to be like for Patty in heaven. "When we get these kind of doubts, I feel that it's Satan knocking on the door," Mel says. "You have to rely on Scripture. We can say by the power and name of Jesus, 'Get out of my life, Satan!' And you must go to Scripture because Scripture says, 'Resist the devil, and he will flee from you' (James 4:7). But you can't leave your mind empty. You must put Scripture in there. That's how I fight my battles."

God gives us great promises from the Bible to stand on and fight the doubts that come from the enemy. Mel points to 1 Corinthians 2:9 which says,

> "However, as it is written:
> What no eye has seen,
> what no ear has heard,
> and what no human mind has conceived"—
> the things God has prepared for those who love him—

Mel thinks about the doubts the Israelites had after God had miraculously freed them from captivity. As they were wandering around in the desert they said, "Why don't we go back to Egypt? At least we had some food to eat there." Mel says, "But God would always bring to mind the great things He had done for them. The same with the disciples. He would tell them, 'Don't you remember when I fed five thousand with a loaf of bread and a few fish? Don't you remember when I walked on water?'"

As Mel faced Patty's homegoing, he remembered God's faithfulness to him through the years and gained great strength through that. "If I can just remember to recall all the things God has done for me in the past, what a help that is! I think about the faith God gave me to give up everything for which I'd worked for twenty-five years – struggling through all the engineering and math stuff in college, rising to an executive position in the steel company, and then, to walk away from it just five or six years until retirement. To say to God, 'There's no reason why You won't be faithful this time.' If things don't come out like I want them, it's because God wants me to learn something through it."

Mel had been in the ministry about ten years, six of them at Denton Bible Church, when he faced a great temptation. He took a trip to Colorado and visited with some of the men from CF&I where he had worked as a top-level executive. The head of the plant said to Mel, "How about coming back? I have a superintendent job for you." After struggling in the ministry without much money, Mel was tempted to take the job. The Scripture that came to mind was Luke 9:62 where Jesus said, "No one who puts a hand to the plow and looks back is fit for service in the kingdom of God." Mel once again walked away from the world's riches to serve his Lord.

The story of the centurion in Luke 7 encourages Mel to walk by faith. "This guy wasn't even Jewish," Mel says. "but he came to Jesus and asked Him to heal his servant. This is the story that Mel loves:

"Now Jesus started on His way with them; and when He was not far from the house, the centurion sent friends, saying to Him, "Lord, do not trouble Yourself further, for I am not worthy for You to come under my roof; for this reason I did not even consider myself worthy to come to You, but just say the word, and my servant will be healed. For I also am a man placed under authority, with soldiers under me; and I say to this one, 'Go!" and he goes, and to another, 'Come!' and he comes, and to my slave, 'Do this!' and he does it." Now when Jesus heard this, He marveled at him, and turned and said to the crowd that was following Him, 'I say to you, not even in Israel have I found such great faith.' When those who had been sent returned to the house, they found the slave in good health. (Luke 7:6-10).

Mel says, "Jesus commended him for his great faith. That's an encouraging thing for me as I've tried to walk by faith. That doesn't mean that my faith doesn't falter at times. That's one of my great struggles. I want to be like Christ. Our testimony to the world is how close are our ways to those of Jesus?

"I went into a restaurant to have lunch today with one of the young men I disciple. There was a lady sitting there with two little girls, and I stopped and said, 'Oh, my, look at these precious children!' She lit up like you can't imagine. I laid my hands on her and said, 'May God bless you and keep you.' That's the kind of thing I envision Jesus doing. I want to try to become like Him on a very practical basis, to have the compassion He had. Jesus said to Jerusalem, 'Jerusalem, Jerusalem, who kills the prophets and stones those who are sent to her. How often I wanted to gather your children together, the way a hen gathers her chicks under her wings, but you were unwilling.' That is our Savior's heart of compassion that He wants us to have."

Mel's favorite verses for dealing with the *past* are Philippians 3:13-14: "Brethren, I do not regard myself as having laid hold of it yet; but one thing I do: *forgetting what lies behind and reaching forward to what lies ahead*, I press on toward the goal for the prize of the upward call of God in Christ Jesus." These verses resonate with Mel because memories of his early struggles still come back to him; growing up in abject poverty, struggling through the Depression, having his father die when he was a teenager, then fighting in World War II as a Marine and picking up shrapnel. His verse for living in the *present* is Philippians 4:13, "I can do all things through Christ who strengthens me." As Mel thinks about the *future*, he's thankful that he's been born again and in the hands of God, trying to serve Him and be obedient to Him.

Mel hasn't slowed down. At age ninety-two, he sometimes wears out his young disciples. Since his sweetheart Patty passed away on June 22, 2017, Mel has taught separate classes for widowers and widows on heaven, continued to disciple several men a week, and developed and taught a leadership course for millennials. He is constantly researching and praying for new ways to make the gospel relevant to young people and to encourage them to use their gifts and talents for the Lord.

Jason Fanning, who teaches at the DBC evening service, relates how the class for millennials came about. "At age ninety-two Mel approached me with one of his plans. (Mel always has a plan for your life.) He said, 'Jason, I want to pour into the next generation before I die. Will you help me gather a small group of men who fall into the Millennial category and help me disciple them? I want to be part of the solution to passing on our faith to the next generation.' Then his genuine humility came out as he said, 'I don't know if I have much to offer them, nor if I can even relate to them. But, if you think it's a good idea, I'd like to try.'

Jason's response was simple, "Mel, the only problem we're going to have is making this group small. The second I mention being personally discipled by Mel, we'll have every young guy in the church lined up. Young guys are dying for men like you to be in their lives." As Mel taught the millennials, he discovered how much they have to offer. "These young people want to be heard," Mel says. "They have gifts and talents that the church needs; they are the future of Denton Bible Church." Mel attends both the Sunday morning and Sunday evening services. Tommy preaches in the Sunday morning services, and the worship, led by Kendall Lucas, includes a choir and an orchestra. Jason Fanning preaches on Sunday evenings, and the worship is led by Nathan McCarter and a praise band. Mel began attending the evening service to get to know the millennials better. He can be found in the foyer at both services surrounded by a group of millennials. Mel's passion for missions still burns deeply in his heart, and he is passing that on to these young men.

Mel's legacy includes the current Denton Bible Church missions department, SERVE, that reaches around the world for Christ. What he started as a sixty-two-year-old continues to thrive.

Chapter 19

SERVE Around the World

Mike Scheer was introduced to Tommy's teaching through cassette tapes when he was part of Fellowship of Christian Athletes in college. When he moved to Denton from his native Kentucky in 1991, he thought he was coming to Denton Bible Church to participate in Tommy's nine-month Young Guns discipleship program. Mike planned to finish the training and then plant churches at the edge of the mountains in Kentucky and Tennessee. However, God had a different plan for his life.

"I was working for a company in Dallas as a business planning consultant and going to seminary," Mike recalls. "I had gone through Young Guns with James Arnold, who came on staff as the Director of Missions at Denton Bible Church in 1994. In 1998, James came to me and said, 'Can you help me think about what missions could be?' We started meeting and in 1999 SERVE originated." Mel had begun to wind down from traveling around the world to take care of his aging mom. Mike joined the missions staff in 1999 and took over as Director of Missions when James moved to France as a missionary in 2007.

Although Mike never traveled with Mel on mission trips, he learned valuable lessons from him. "Mel is compassionate and gracious to people, but he never coddles them," Mike says. "He walks a fine line between hugging and loving on people and challenging them to do great things. He has a way of motivating people to do things they would not have done otherwise and doing it in a way where they feel encouraged and built up. I've never seen that in anybody else."

Mike told a story that demonstrates Mel's devotion to missions. "I can remember him being in the hospital years ago. I walked in, and he had his eyes closed, so I thought he must be asleep. I thought, 'I'll pray quietly and go.' I was getting ready to leave, and he said, with his eyes still closed, 'What are you doing in the Solomon Islands?' Here he is laying in a hospital bed, and his first thought is 'What ministry are you doing in the Solomon Islands?' His mind, his heart is still around the world. That's Mel."

Mel has big visions, but he takes his commitment to family seriously. One of Mike's most enduring memories of Mel is him stepping down to take care of his mother. Mike says, "Mel also stepped down to take care of Patty. I saw him pushing Patty in that wheelchair at church; that's Mel. He took care of both his mother and wife well."

Chris Cobble, *BTCP* Coordinator, works with Mike at SERVE. He says, "In many ways I owe Mel my ministry. I was raised in churches that had no discipleship, and the pastors didn't have any training. I was 22 when I came to Texas in 1997, a wide-eyed young man looking to go to seminary and do Young Guns so I could go back and train pastors in east Tennessee."

Chris felt overwhelmed at the thought of training pastors, uncertain where to begin. When he came to Denton people said, "You need to meet Mel Sumrall and investigate what he's doing." Chris remembers, "I started hearing about *BTCP*, and I realized that it wasn't approximately what I was looking for; it was exactly what I needed to go back to East Tennessee to train pastors." However, Mel and James challenged Chris and told him, "It's not just East Tennessee, it's pastors around the world that need this training." Chris now leads the *BTCP* training throughout the world.

Chris recognizes that he doesn't have the gift of starting things. He says, "I'm so thankful for Mel's initiative in traveling to hear Bill Bright, and not just coming away with 'that's a big need,' but 'I've got to do something about it.' He took the initiative when it was uncomfortable. Because he did, I'm in ministry today."

Chris says, "I read a lot of biographies of great men, and Mel has that same fire. It's a vision of this big mission. Mel calls us all to a greater vision for the Lord's work. That's always an encouragement to me. It's like I hear his voice in the back of my head sometimes, pushing us as far as he can push us."

Mel pushes, but there's a flip side. Chris says, "How many girls lived with them, how many men has he met with weekly? Most of the guys that have Mel's 'gift-mix' as a visionary don't get along with people. In Mel, you've got this guy that makes you uncomfortable with big ideas, but he does it in the context of community and loving people and relationships. When Mel comes in, I don't take him as some arbitrary guy that makes me uncomfortable for uncomfortable sake. He loves me and is concerned about me."

Janis Saville came on staff as the Missions Women Director in 2013. Prior to that she worked closely with the missions office, often putting in sixty hours a week as a volunteer. She began doing that in 2001 when James Arnold told her, "This is what you're going to do." Janis says, "I did a variety of things to promote women's missionary activities, whether long-term missionaries or short-term mission trips. Prior to that, I had done short-term trips with *Titus 2 International*. I took my first mission trip with Barbara McGee to Kenya for a month in 1995 where *BTCP* had already started. We taught the first edition of *Titus 2* which hadn't been fully written at that time."

Mel models for Janis something that still enlivens what she does. "I'm not as old as Mel, but I went to seminary late in life. Seeing what he did gave me the impetus to continue." Mel also inspired Janis with his vision for reaching out to the world. Janis said, "It's hard for me to think about doing ministry without having a big map in my mind, always thinking about other places we can go. Plus, from the very beginning, it was inspiring for me to hear Mel speak about the need for ministry to women. He would come up to me and say, 'You need to get out there and train these women and have them go to the villages.' As a woman, it was good to have that encouragement and to hear Mel say that."

Mel hasn't only inspired Mike, Chris, and Janis individually, but Mike sees Mel's fingerprints on everything done at Denton Bible

Church. He says, "When God teaches Mel a lesson through the experiences, struggles and challenges in life, he passes that on. We are who we are as a church largely because of who he is."

That statement resonates with Tommy as he reflects on Mel and the history of Denton Bible Church.

Chapter 20

Tommy's Reflections

Tommy was at the DFW airport one day when he ran into Ned Wilson, a pilot for Pan Am. Ned was coming in from a flight, and when he saw Tommy he came over and said, "I went to a church meeting at the Optimist Gym. There's a fellow there about my age named Mel Sumrall. You're about half his age, but you and he are thinking the same thing. I told him about you. You two ought to get together." Mel and Tommy met at Denny's in a corner booth by the window in front. After all these years, Tommy still remembers the booth.

"Mel was a Dallas (Dallas Theological Seminary) guy, and I was a Dallas guy," Tommy says. "He didn't mean to be in ministry. God just took him out of the business world. I didn't mean to be in ministry. God took me out of football. Mel had been a track, cross-country guy, and I was a football player. He had kids, and I had just had a kid. Our spirits were the same."

Tommy remembers he and a guy named Greg Talkington going to Mel and Patty's house for dinner. Soon after that, Mel had a talk with the elders and got their approval to offer Tommy a job. Mel met with Tommy and said, "Why don't you come with us?"

"Can you pay me anything?" Tommy asked him. "They came up with four hundred dollars a month," says Tommy. "Mel was in the big money; he made six hundred dollars a month." Tommy was now officially on staff at Denton Bible Church.

The only house Tommy and Teresa could find was a rent house next door to Mel on Selene Street. Fond memories of those days linger in Tommy's mind. "When we lived next door to one another on Selene Street, I'd walk next door and we would sit and drink coffee and dream about what God could do. A lot of things came out of our dreams. That was a sweet time. I still drive by those little houses on Selene Street."

Mel and Tommy would also drive out to Tommy's father-in-law's place in East Texas and spend the night at the lake house there. The juices would start flowing, and they would start dreaming, never imagining what Denton Bible Church would look like forty years later. Prayer has been a top priority at DBC since its beginning. Tommy read about Dawson Trotman, founder of Navigators, praying for forty days. He and Mel began meeting every morning at 4 a.m. at Mel's house to pray for the church. "I'd go over to his house, and Mel would come out in his pajamas," Tommy says. "Patty was still asleep. He and I would pray for two hours. We made it thirty-two days when Mel got pneumonia. I kid people and say, 'No telling how great DBC would be if Mel hadn't gotten sick!'"

Denton Bible's Sunday evening service was actually a prayer meeting. Mel and Tommy would get the guys in one of their homes, and the girls in the other house, and they would pray for revival. "God moved us toward prayer," Tommy says. God answered the prayers of Mel, Tommy and the members of Denton Bible Church in an incredible way.

Tommy adds to Mel's memories of clearing the land for the first building. "It had never been touched," he says. "I went out on the land and came back and said to Mel and the elders, 'There's no way you can clear this land. We'll have to hire a bulldozer.' But we began to go out on Saturday mornings and work until about two o'clock. We would take machetes and chain saws and rakes. Jack George had a flatbed truck, so we would take the briars and the branches and put them on the flatbed and take them to the dump. With all of us working, it wasn't too long until the land was cleared, and we had a place for a church and parking lot. My son Benjamin was about six years old, and he came with me.

"We built the church ourselves. We had a bricklayer in the church that laid the brick. Nolan Barnett was the general contractor. We had to pay for the steel, but we did the rest of it. We put up the sheetrock ourselves. I can show you where I was when I poured in insulation. That's where I met Jim Hill; together we put up a piece of sheetrock. Then, the girls would come out and fix lunch at noon. We got that thing up! Our first Sunday was on Easter in 1982, and we had about 135 people. The ceiling wasn't even finished; we had bare bulbs hanging down."

Tommy reflects on how he and Mel complemented each other with their gifts. "Preaching wasn't Mel's strength; it wasn't easy for him. I would get criticized for being too doctrinal, and Mel would get criticized sometimes for his teaching. Some Christians can be so insensitive. One time a pilot who attended Denton Bible set up a meeting with Mel and basically criticized him. Mel is sensitive, and it hurt him. Mel was discouraged and wanted to give up. I would literally go pick him up and say, 'You're going with me,' and take him to prayer meetings and stuff."

Tommy had his times of discouragement. He says, "Our roughest year was 1984. It was my fault, because I'd taught a group of young people and singles, without requiring ministry and evangelism of them as I should have. We just turned out a great bunch of minds with no heart. We had to discipline an elder's wife, because she left him and wouldn't tell us why. This group of people really didn't like it. They were more into congregational rule. After that church meeting, they stormed out. It was the closest we had to a split. It wasn't the leadership, it was just those people. They all went tepid.

"It really hit me. I thought, 'If I can't do any better than this, I need to go coach somewhere.' I was extremely down, and Mel kept me going. He would make me go eat with him at Wyatt's Cafeteria. God comforted my soul. He was with me. It was right after that, Jack George was leading music in the Sumrall Center, and those people had left. I got ready to get up to preach, and Jack looked at me. He handed me the one lapel microphone we had, and he said, 'Fresh wind,' because they were gone. It's like God said, 'If y'all are willing to stand by My Word, I'll stand by you.'"

Through the ups-and-downs, Mel and Tommy supported one another. Tommy says, "Denton Bible would have done no good with Mel by himself. Denton Bible wouldn't have done good with me by myself. We were like a blind guy pushing a paraplegic in a wheelchair. He was my eyes; I was his legs."

From 1984 to 1990, Denton Bible grew to about seven hundred people with three services on Sunday. Somewhere around 1990, Tommy went jogging with DBC member, Jimmy Rench. He said to Tommy, "You know what you ought to preach? Song of Solomon." Tommy had previously taught it in small groups, and it was extremely popular. Tommy said, "We'd have a riot." Jimmy Rench replied, "You might be surprised."

Tommy went to Gruber in the Texas panhandle where he had some friends. He told them he was going to teach Song of Solomon to their church on Friday night and Saturday morning. He taught it, and they loved it. Tommy thought, "If these old guys from Gruber First Baptist can handle it, our church body can handle it." He began teaching the Song of Solomon, and Denton Bible went from seven hundred to twelve hundred people in six weeks. Tommy realized he had found the Mother Lode. Denton Bible Church had taken off. On Sundays, cars would park in the ditch, the culvert, the woods, everywhere. Everybody said, "This church is here to stay."

Tommy says of Mel, "The great thing Mel could do was start programs. Mel attended Reinhardt Bible Church in Dallas before he moved to Denton. Reinhardt Bible had a big influence on us. Dale Hamilton, who attended Reinhardt Bible, brought a guy from there to talk to us elders about Evangelism Explosion. This guy was so passionate about it that Mel called D. James Kennedy's church in Coral Ridge, Florida where E.E. originated, to find out about it. Mel took three others and attended training in E.E. in Oklahoma.

Tommy remarks, "If it weren't for Mel, I would have stayed within my comfort zone—which would have been education—and we would currently have a five hundred person Bible church that's highly educated. Mel was great at being the Apostle Paul. He would get things going and give it to someone else. *Unleashing the Church* was Mel. *Navigator's 2:7* was Mel. *E.E.* was Mel. *BTCP* was Mel. The overseas work was Mel. He would pioneer things. He had all kinds of ideas for outreach. I had to trust God in areas that weren't strengths to me. We always went together. Anytime we did something, it was he and I together. We were a united front."

Tommy talks about the greatest lessons he's learned from Mel. "He never had a private life and a public life. He had integrity in everything he did. He always treated Patty like a queen. It was an inspiration to me. He had real endurance. Trials with kids. Patty's illness. Still today, his mind is always cooking. As soon as Patty was buried, Mel thought, 'I'm going to do a ministry to widowers.'"

Tommy and Mel have spent the best years of their lives with one another. Tommy says, "He took me at one of the hardest places of my life, when I had to leave the Methodist church. He was there. At the hardest place in my ministry, he was there. In the formation of my marriage, he was there. He was good friends with my father. My daddy liked him; my mama liked him. He is closer than a brother. He's like a father."

When Mel stepped down from staff at age seventy-five, Tommy had some concerns about being able to run the elder board. Tommy was forty-something when Mel stepped down, and most of the men on the elder board were sixty-something. Tommy says, "I always thought, 'If I have to run this place myself, I'm going to end up killing somebody.' Mel was always kind of the prow of the ship. But I found out that God could give me grace. I hate conflict. I like to keep things peaceful. But I found out that I was the prince of darkness. I had to be. I found out that there were guys that crossed the line. I would go to bed a lamb and wake up a lion. I found out I could do that. It was unnerving at first because I had always worked with college students. These were guys older than me. But God gave me grace."

When Patty died, Tommy got up to speak about her. He says, "I've done a million funerals. But this was so hard. Patty was a gentle soul. I never saw Patty mad. When their daughter died, Patty took it in stride. Mel went into a two-year depression. You could hit Patty with anything, and she would stay on course."

However, if not for Mel and Patty losing little Pamela, and consequently Mel's depression, Denton Bible Church might not have existed. Romans 8:28 has been proven true in Mel and Tommy's lives. God does work all things together for good for those who love Him and are called according to His purpose. Mel and Tommy have each suffered and endured hardship for the sake of Denton Bible Church. God took two opposites and brought them together to do a mighty work for His kingdom. After forty years of ministry together, Mel and Tommy's hearts and souls are knit together in love for one another.

Chapter 21

Memories from Sumrall Children

Susan Sumrall

Susan grew up loving the water. During the Korean War, Mel was stationed at Camp Pendleton, located along the southern coast of California. Trips to the beach were common, and one of Susan's favorite pastimes was digging up cigarette butts at the beach. "I was about two years old," Susan said, "and Mom and Dad took pictures of me doing that."

In addition to swimming, Susan loved skiing with her family when they moved back to Colorado after the war. Mel and Patty took the kids on summer vacations to historical sites such as the Cliff Dwellings. One summer the family visited the Mormon Tabernacle and listened to the choir rehearse Handel's Messiah. Susan remembers driving across country to visit Patty's mom and dad in Pennsylvania. "I really enjoyed the greener countryside and the humidity of the east coast which was such a contrast to the Colorado mesa."

Her memories of her mom's cooking include the spaghetti and meatballs that she made. Susan said, "There were a lot of Italians in our rural neighborhood, and I don't know who she got the recipe from, but it was phenomenal!" Mel and Patty raised their own steers for several years, and Patty would fix roast, hamburgers, and meat-loaf using the good quality beef from their steers. In addition, Patty made plum jam from the plums that grew along the irrigation ditch and prepared corn and other vegetables to freeze that the family grew on their acre of land. Patty set an example of what healthy eating looked like. Patty was a "no sugar" person. Susan said, "I got my first taste of sugar when I was five years old and was given a sucker at the pediatrician's office."

From an early age, Susan had issues with speaking. Susan says, "I had severe stuttering issues into adulthood. Also, I grew up in an era where women were not important to listen to. It could have been a combination of all those things, but I didn't really have a voice until I reached adulthood. Most of the time I didn't speak. It was tough navigating life and not having a voice and having to depend on somebody else to know what I wanted to communicate."

Mel and Patty were at a loss at what to do. They wanted to get Susan into counseling, but it was difficult to do that in those days. Susan said, "I had trouble getting my school work done in high school because it was hard for me to focus. I finally got help in my early twenties from a psychologist who gave me a metronome to wear in my ear. That helped me begin to have a rhythm in my speech and to be able to complete sentences."

In addition to struggling with her speech, twelve-year-old Susan felt distressed for her dad when baby Pamela died. Susan remembers, "Dad would go in Pamela's room and just sob. Watching that, I took that on myself, and I tried to carry that burden for him. When a child sees a parent like that, you think they're going to die. You want to do whatever you can to help. A lot of that time I don't have any memories, just a lot of grief."

During Susan's difficulties, she received Jesus as Lord around the age of eight. "Mom took us to church from an early age," Susan said. "We went to a little church called Grace Community Church where I went to Sunday school." The biggest thing that has impacted Susan's life is the unconditional love she received from Mel and Patty. She said, "Everyone goes through heartache and trauma growing up. I always felt that if I had to come home or wanted to, they would always welcome me with open arms and not be critical. They were both always wanting to help me solve issues or problems that I had."

Susan continued, "One of the most amazing things about Mom and Dad is their diligence in serving God, having their lives be a testimony to His saving grace. Mom was always loving, warm and kind. She was positive, always lifting us up and lifting up other people around us."

In 2009 Susan moved in with Mel and Patty. "Mom was starting to have some memory issues," Susan said. "Earlier in her life she had broken both wrists. She had major osteoporosis issues. I'm so grateful that I had the opportunity to be with Mom and Dad during the last eight years to help minister to her. I feel like the Lord opened the door for me to stay with them. They basically rescued me. I was having to start over again for the zillionth time, and they took me in. I immediately started to help Mom. I feel blessed to be with Dad right now. He's always put a lot of effort into doing what he can to stay healthy. He's still doing that as he continues to disciple men and teach classes."

Susan said, "I've been able to restore and rebuild and be in a place I haven't been before in my life, and it's exciting. This is a joyful time for me because I'm getting to do what I'm passionate about. I have one parent that's not in heaven yet, and my family is here close by. I haven't been around my family for 30 years because I was living in Hawaii."

God is teaching Susan precious things about her walk with Him, and she is looking forward to the opportunities He has for her to serve in the future.

Jerry Sumrall

Jerry Robert Sumrall was born in Pueblo, Colorado on January 21, 1954. He says, "My mom was the epitome of kindness, and my dad was kind of macho. He loved the mountains and camping. I remember our vacations always included a river where we would fly fish; I loved that."

Jerry remembers his mom and dad looking for ways to challenge him and his siblings to prepare them for the future. "For example, in high school I passionately wanted a Yamaha dirt bike. Mom and Dad were literally building our house in the country by hand. Dad said, 'Son, we will pay for half of it, but you must work out the remainder by helping us build our home.' I did that and learned carpentry, plumbing, meager details about electrical wiring, and brick laying." Jerry appreciates that he has saved a bundle of money by doing his own home repairs.

Jerry says, "When I was a child Mom and Dad began taking us to Sunday school and church at Grace Community Church. I looked forward to summer Bible camps at Camp Iana in the Colorado mountains. I received Christ at an early age at my church."

Jerry has worked as an engineer in fiber optics with NEC for thirty years. Jerry graduated from LeTourneau University and spent some time at Wheaton College. He's married to Audrey, an elementary school teacher. They have two children, Kaylee and Nathan. Both have followed in Jerry's footsteps, graduating from LeTourneau University. Nathan got an engineering degree like his dad. Kaylee has a toddler named Jack.

Karen Clopton

Karen drew her first breath on January 3, 1955. She was Mel and Patty's third child. Karen is married to Guy, and they have a son named Jonathan. Karen and Guy live in Gladewater, about fifteen miles from Longview.

Karen says, "My favorite childhood memories with Mom and Dad would be the summer vacations and winter ski trips they took us on. They took us to so many places in the United States. They were very involved in whatever we were doing." She appreciates Mel and Patty working hard to provide for the needs of the family. "I remember Mom sewing our clothes when I was young, especially Easter dresses. She did such a beautiful job," Karen says.

"I had a wonderful and blessed life growing up" Karen reflects. "God is always good in everything. Any difficulties came from my own perception or desires. Most would have thought it'd be the death of my little sister, but I don't really remember it. The only thing I remember is where we sat at the funeral." Even though little Pamela's death drew Mel into depression, he and Patty did their best to help their children through it.

Karen loves her dad's dedication to God and to his family. She loved her mom's heart of thankfulness to God and others for everything. "I also loved her dry sense of humor," Karen says. Karen's relationship with Jesus was greatly influenced by Mel and Patty's dedication to Him. "They trusted Him for everything, and that increased my desire to want the same," Karen remembers.

Laura Pauline Villegas

As the youngest child, Laura felt safe at home with her parents and within the family. She says, "My dad's undying love and dedication for our mother trickled down to all of us. We all felt we were his favorite, and we still do." Watching her mom's love for her dad inspired Laura. "I watched their Christian marriage," Laura says, "and how they flourished in life with the Lord by their side. I wanted that peace, as well."

In addition, Laura remembers the influence her mother had on her young mind. "My mom introduced me to movies like *Heidi* and bought me records of *Hansel and Gretel* that broadened my imagination." Mel's love of fly fishing left Laura with wonderful memories as the family traveled to Montana and other places. Mel and Patty took Laura, along with the other children, to church every week and made sure they were involved in camps, Sunday school, and other church activities.

However, even growing up in a home with loving parents like Mel and Patty doesn't guarantee a struggle-free life. Laura, in her honesty, shares the following: "When I was young, I could decipher between good and bad influences, but I couldn't stand either side being upset with me. I would take the blame of wrongdoings of my "friends," thus portraying a negative picture of myself sometimes. This was the hardest part of my childhood. I felt I was disappointing everyone. "I married at nineteen and when my husband made disapproving comments, I thought it was normal. I didn't understand how this most intimate relationship molded me into a person without a voice or backbone."

Laura has become a strong person through her struggles. She has regrets, but also gratefulness for her dad's continued support. "In my new marriage and in my recently diagnosed terminal cancer, Dad has been there," Laura says. "It's not only with marriages that we make the vow 'in sickness and in health.' It also includes our children."

Mel is there for his children.

Chapter 22

Patty
Mel's Sweetheart and
the Love of His Life

On February 20, 2011, Tommy Nelson honored Patty Sumrall in the Denton Bible Church services. He said in part, "She has been a 'help suitable' for Mel in grace and dignity. We take this Valentine's season to thank and honor Denton Bible's sweetheart and the woman behind the man. . .Patty Sumrall."

Patty was Mel's sweetheart for seventy years and ten months, but she was also loved and cherished by the members of Denton Bible Church. Her gentle, caring ways will long be remembered. Her love, faithfulness to Mel, and support in the ministry shines as an example of a godly wife. Mel credits his ability to go forth in ministry, both at Denton Bible Church and around the world, largely to Patty.

"It's important for a husband and wife to be a team," Mel says. "If Patty had said 'no' to me going to seminary, I wouldn't have gone. If she had said 'no' to foreign missions, I wouldn't have gone. I didn't want to be away from her. But she was always by my side; she went where I went."

This chapter is dedicated to Patty, who passed away on June 22, 2017. As the woman behind the man, her influence continues to touch lives around the world. Mel states that he couldn't have been used by God in so many ways without the encouragement and faith of Patty. Here is Patty's story.

Vivian Jones Ross and Robert L. Ross welcomed little Patricia Louise Sumrall into the world on July 30, 1925. She had a sister, Jeannie, who was blonde and shy, and a brother named Bobby. Patty's father graduated from University of Colorado in Boulder with a degree in Electrical Engineering. After graduation, he and Vivian moved to Pittsburgh, Pennsylvania where he worked for Westinghouse Electric. When it was time for Patty's birth, Vivian returned to Colorado so she could be with her mother, known as Grandma Jones. Although the Great Depression hit shortly after Patty was born, it didn't affect the Ross family like it did many American families. Because Patty's dad worked for Westinghouse Electric, the family had luxuries such as an electric stove, refrigerator, and a phone when many Americans were suffering through poverty. During World War II, unknown to the family, Robert Ross worked on the Manhattan Project. They later found out that the atom bombs dropped on Japan were a result of the Manhattan Project. He also worked on America's tallest concrete dam, Hoover Dam, when it was being built from 1931 to 1936.

Patty's mother, Vivian Ross, played the piano for church and for silent films. Vivian was often sick, and Patty helped take care of her. Patty attended Township High School in Murraysville, Pennsylvania where her favorite class was sewing. She learned to make all her clothes including wool jackets and skirts which would be a skill Patty would use when she had children and money was short.

Patty moved back to Pueblo to attend Pueblo Junior College where her cousin Shirley Ann Tappan was a student. Once Shirley Ann introduced Mel to Patty, he would scope out social activities at college and make dates ahead of time so no one else could ask her out. Patty never dated anyone but Mel once they were introduced. Mel knew this was the woman for him. He had been working part-time at the steel mill and was able to save for an engagement ring. Mel and Patty had plans to go to a formal dance, so Mel took the ring and put it in the corsage box. "She was amazed," Mel says. "I asked her if she would marry me, and she said 'yes.'"

Patty wore a pale blue taffeta wedding dress that she made herself and a simple headdress made by Shirley Ann. Mel and Patty received one gift for their wedding; twenty-five dollars from her dad. After their wedding in a Presbyterian church in Pennsylvania, the happy couple left for their honeymoon in Niagara Falls. The twenty-five dollars from her dad, which was a lot of money in 1946, paid for their honeymoon and got them back to Colorado.

While they attended Pueblo Junior College, Patty and Mel lived in an apartment on East 7th Street in Pueblo that was owned by Shirley Tappan's grandfather. Two years later, they both graduated with their associate's degrees. The young couple moved to Boulder, and Mel enrolled at the University of Colorado. Part of the university housing included a trailer park called 'Vetsville.' (All the students were veterans.) Mel and Patty lived in a twenty-foot trailer while Mel went to school, and Patty took care of many children to support them. Their first child, Susan, was born six weeks before Mel graduated.

After graduation, Mel worked as a metallurgist at CF&I, sometimes working twenty-four hours straight if problems developed at the mill. Mel remembers his boss, Clay Crawford saying to him, "I'm going to transfer into production management, and I have to have someone at my right hand who will be loyal to me. You're my choice." Mel's loyalty paid off, and he continued to rise in the company along with Clay Crawford.

Patty's involvement with the Girl Scouts as a child instilled her with a love for the outdoors which dovetailed with Mel's outdoor activities. Eventually Jerry, Karen, Laura and Pamela were born. Mel and Patty took the kids camping all over Colorado, Wyoming, and Montana in a little trailer. When they were fishing on the Gunnison River, they made harnesses and tied the kids together and then tied them to the bushes to keep them from falling in the river. Jerry was especially challenging because he wanted to climb all the time. Fish were plentiful, and the family often had fried fish for breakfast and sometimes for dinner.

After the tragedy of little Pamela's passing, life changed dramatically for the Sumrall family. As Mel explained in a previous chapter, the Lord used Ron Chadwick to disciple him through his two years of depression. Knowing that God was calling him into the ministry, Mel moved the family to Dallas to attend Dallas Theological Seminary.

The rest is history. Mel started Denton Bible Church in 1976 with Patty at his side. God sent Tommy and Teresa Nelson in the fall of 1977 to serve with Mel and Patty. Teresa shares her memories of Patty. "We had been married three years, and Benjamin was a year and a half old when we moved next door to Mel and Patty on Selene Street. We lived there for two years until we bought a house on Malone Street."

Teresa remembers her first impression of Patty. "She was very sweet, kind and gentle. She loved children. Patty taught kindergarten and was drawn to kids. That's why she enjoyed Benjamin so much. She loved my child." The often-told story of Benjamin coming to the fence and calling Patty is one of Teresa's fond memories of Patty. "We wouldn't let him call Mel by his first name, so we told him, 'This is Mr. Mel.' Benjamin decided it was Mr. Mel, Mr. Pat, and their cat was Mr. Joe Cat." This is Teresa's favorite story about Patty because it shows that she was thinking of others all the time. Teresa says, "Was she busy doing something else when Benjamin came to the fence? Probably. Her hair was in curlers. But Ben's out there going, 'Mr. Pat, Mr. Pat.' She would stop and minister to Benjamin—whether he needed it or not."

Teresa remembers Patty as very thoughtful, methodical, and deliberate about everything she did. "I think that's why she was a really good teacher," Teresa says. She remembers Patty's infectious laugh. "When she got tickled, it was like a kid getting tickled. A precious laughter, pure and genuine. There was no phoniness in Patty. She was courteous, kind, sympathetic, just a gentle lady."

Teresa and Patty both had the same goal – to help their husbands be successful in leading Denton Bible Church. With mainly college students in the early years of DBC, there wasn't much money to support Mel and Tommy and the church. One of Patty's huge contributions in helping Mel establish Denton Bible was her willingness to work the first nine years of DBC at Trinity Christian Academy in north Dallas.

With Patty working and commuting, it was difficult for her put a lot of time into ministry at DBC. That left Teresa to initiate women's Bible studies. "I was twenty-seven years old, and I was one of the older people," Teresa said. "I started Bible studies and developing women's groups before Barbara McGee, because she was a fairly young Christian at that point. Eventually, Barbara was appointed as the first director of women's ministry."

Tommy and Teresa also hosted college groups at their home. "It was different for Patty because she was working, and she commuted every day," Teresa says. "We didn't lead studies together. Patty was confident with children, but she wasn't as confident leading women, but she did it. She knew she had to push herself out of her comfort zone. She did mentor girls in her way. She was methodical. She planned it out."

Patty also taught kids in Sunday school. Teresa remembers the weird Sunday school situations when DBC began. "When we met at the Optimist Gym, the nursery was a broom closet for my baby John and a kid from Nigeria. The bar was where the other Sunday schools met. Bob Boso was one of our first Sunday school teachers. One Sunday two-year-old Ben goes in there riding his imaginary horse and says, 'Give me a veer (beer).' He didn't know what he was saying. He'd seen a bar on TV where they served beer. Patty also taught Sunday school when the church met at Camp Copas. We were in dorm rooms with bunk beds; it was a nightmare controlling children in a bunk bed situation.

"Those were joyful years in the beginning of Denton Bible Church," Teresa recalls. "Our kids were at an age when it was fun. Building the first building was fun and joyful. Everybody pitched in together. The college kids totally invested into the body. They came to learn, be part, and contribute. Fun years when we'd say, 'We're going skiing.' I'd plan and get all the food we'd take with us, and we would go to Red River or wherever. It was a younger crowd that participated in everything going on at Denton Bible Church. It was a sweet time of life."

Most of the time, Mel and Patty went skiing with Tommy and Teresa and the young crowd. Patty was a great skier, but Teresa remembers how fragile she was. "Patty had broken bones from skiing, from stepping on a pine cone and falling down. She was fragile but very tough and energetic." Teresa saw great strength in Patty. "She had emotional stability, calmness, and was methodical. That stability made her dependable. A rock. It's what enabled her to do what she had to do. I believe that's why she carried their family when Pam died. I always saw that stability in her. She thought through what to do next. She was emotionally tough, but just looking at her and talking to her you wouldn't think that."

From Patty, Teresa learned to demonstrate consideration and thoughtfulness not only towards adults, but also towards little children. "I learned from Patty to get down on their level and talk to them like a regular person. I still do that," Teresa says. Patty was faithful and never complained. Teresa says, "I never heard her say anything bad about anyone. She was just a good person. Patty was behind the scenes, but she lived out all aspects of the 'love one anothers' we have in the Bible. We are to "accept one another," we "defer to one another," we "greet one another." Patty was good at greeting. She was happy. Even when she had Alzheimer's she would say, 'Oh, Teresa.' She recognized how valued a person felt when they were warmly greeted. That was Patty."

The following are memories from people who spoke at Patty's memorial service on June 26, 2017.

Kay Myers

"I got to know Patty in 1987 when I started working in the church office. She was a tough and tender lady. As I watched her travel all over the world with Mel, I'm reminded of Ruth in the Old Testament. Ruth left her family and everything familiar to go with Naomi and Naomi's God. This was Patty to Mel. At a time when most folks begin to settle in and seek a quieter life, this tough and tender lady never faltered in her commitment to the Lord and to her husband, both of whom she loved deeply. Patty was tender in spirit to the very end." Kay describes Patty as having a sparkle in her eye and a song and smile on her lips to the very end, even though Alzheimer's had taken its toll. "She will be greatly missed," Kay says.

Vonnie George

Patty was a true Christian, and she had an essence about her. She was plugged into the Holy Spirit, and you could hear it in her words and in her attitude. When I met Patty in 1981, I knew I was meeting a truly godly woman, someone who could teach me to be a godly wife. She was wise and gentle in spirit. The Lord just spilled out of her and onto other people.

"Mel deeply trusted her. All those trips all over the world were her devotion to him and to the Lord. I think she regained strength from serving others. It says in Proverbs 31 that an excellent wife does good all the days of her life. Patty did that to her last breath. It was amazing to watch Patty. Her physical strength failed, but her spiritual strength never failed. Her dedication was not only to the man who was fully devoted to her, but also to her children and to us, the church body. You could feel it when you were in her presence."

Patty loved singing hymns and did so almost to the end. "I sat beside Patty and listened to her singing hymns. This godly woman poured out her spirit, and I could feel her love for the Lord as she sang."

James Arnold

"I met Patty in 1988, and she was the woman behind the man. I got to see Patty in dozens of countries. I'd come down in the morning, and she'd be humming, singing, and happy—always happy. She'd be sorting out her and Mel's vitamins as she greeted me. Mel and I would be talking about something theological and the ministry for that day, and Patty would be talking about the ministry as well. She'd continually say, 'They just need Jesus.' She'd contribute to the ministry, and she'd point to Jesus with her life and her words.

"I remember we were in Moscow in 1992. This was before you could stay wherever you wanted to, so all the foreigners were put in the Cosmos Hotel. I was single and put in a room by myself. Across the hall was a brothel. When an American or foreigner checked in, the phone would ring across the hall, and a girl would scurry out to promote what she was promoting. As a single guy, I was fearful of my ministry, so I put a chair up against my door and tried to get some sleep.

"In the morning, as Patty sorted vitamins and hummed, she asked me, 'How did you sleep, brother?' I said, 'Not too well. The phone was ringing, girls were coming and going all the time.' She looked at me and delightfully said, 'Why didn't you do what we did? We just invited them in and shared Jesus with them.' That was her heart. She went, she saw, she knew God, and she clung to Him.

"Patty always pointed people to Jesus because they needed Him. If Patty could say something to you today, it would be, 'You just need Jesus. Cling to Jesus.'"

Tommy

"I watched Patty for over forty years. I met her in 1977 at their house on Selene Street. She was always an enigma to me. She was frail. I was afraid to hug her; I might break something, or she'd snap. She was small and quiet and soft and innocent. I never heard her raise her voice.

"In another sense, Patty was superhuman. She endured things in life and she took them with grace, including the death of their baby daughter. She was flawless. In forty years I cannot tell you one flaw in Patty Sumrall. I never saw her raise her voice. I never saw her critical. I never saw her harsh. I never saw her unloving. I never saw her unsupportive. I never saw her frantic. She was enigmatic to be that small and yet that strong in all walks of life. I never saw anything but steadfastness.

"When they lost Pamela at ten months, it brought Mel to his knees. He blamed himself. This World War II marine felt he couldn't take care of his family. In his depression, he would lay on the carpet, and Patty would play the piano to comfort him. She stood by him as he worked through his pain.

"Mel walked away from a big figure income at a steel company to go to seminary, and Patty stood by him. Patty never blinked. When you start a church. . .it can be painful. A wife feels what her husband feels. Teresa and Patty were like these two pillars that stood beside us. Patty was always the encourager, always steadfast, never a bitter word. When I first started my career and preached the best I could, she would always come up to me and tell me how incredible I was.

"Later, Mel would turn his gaze to foreign fields to train pastors around the world, and Patty was there. When you see pictures of Mel in all those places, Patty is always there. When age took its toll, she pressed on. She was never hurried, never out of control. She was careful that the words of her mouth and the meditations of her heart 'were acceptable in Thy sight, Lord, our rock and our strength.' Never did I see her break in forty years. She was an excellent wife, an excellent mother, an excellent employee of Trinity Christian Academy. She was a friend to my wife. In every step there was grace in Patty.

"Yet you could have gone to this church all your life, and you would never have known who she was unless someone pointed her out to you. She was always the wind beneath the wings. That was Patty. Her faith was simple. It was childlike. She trusted in Christ alone and the Bible alone. It was faith that was evidenced by continual faithfulness."

Memories of Patty from the Mission Field

<u>Warren Nystrom</u>

Sitting next to Mel in his living room, Warren talks about memories of Patty. He remembers the love Patty had for Mel, and the love she had for those on the mission trips. "She was so genuine in that love," Warren says. "From the time we knew her in the beginning, she demonstrated receiving you as a friend in Christ. She was so easy to be with. She lived out what she taught. . .how a Christian wife should be. Others would see that, not just me, but everybody on the mission field and in church.

"Patty was so outgoing and so friendly. She always looked around at people and went to give them a hug. Her support for Mel was vital to his ministry. If it wasn't for Patty allowing God to move Mel and the family from Colorado to Dallas for seminary, I wouldn't be sitting here."

<u>Margaret Ashmore</u>

"You can't talk about Mel without talking about Patty because of the mystery and wonder of them being one. I never talked to Patty on any level—casual or otherwise—that she didn't quote Scripture, that she didn't point me to the cross, that she didn't encourage my heart. The thing I'll always remember about Patty is that no matter how diminished her body was, her spirit was stronger. No matter how much her dementia progressed, Patty never forgot the hymns, never forgot Scripture. No matter how incapacitated she was, she always sang praises to God. She loved those hymns. She had a beautiful, lilting voice. When she sang, you'd be lifted.

"Patty was never, ever self-focused. She never complained. It was always about you and how she could encourage you. I'm happy for Patty, because she is receiving her great reward. I'm sad for Mel who misses her, but oh, the great reunion that's coming! There was nothing complicated about Patty. She lived for the simplicity of the gospel. There was nothing that was hard to figure out about her. She lived for Christ, and that was all that mattered to her. She loved her husband. Dedicated. Whenever you saw Mel, Patty was right there. I love Patty, and I look forward to seeing her again one day."

Chapter 23

Mel's Tribute to Patty – Words from Mel

Patty Lou: God's committed servant, my faithful and devoted helper during our seventy plus years together.

We live in a day and age when marriage vows given before the Lord are easily tossed aside as insignificant and meaningless. When I was attending seminary, there was a couple that was having serious problems in their marriage. The wife told her husband, "I don't want to be the wife of a pastor. I will stay with you in this marriage until you graduate from seminary, and then I'm leaving. And that's what she did.

In contrast to this couple, I'd like to describe the many times my beloved and I made major decisions, vowing to stay together and serve Christ—no matter what.

My sweetheart and I graduated from the local community college in Pueblo, Colorado in 1947, and we had been accepted at the University of Colorado. Our source of income at the time was about seventy-five dollars a month on the G.I. Bill. This was not going to pay for the necessities for our last two years of college. What to do? I was enrolled in the College of Mechanical Engineering and would need to average eighteen hours to graduate in two years. This meant I wouldn't have time to work to supplement our income.

I reluctantly said, "Patty Lou, would you be so kind and considerate as to drop out of college and get a job to support us for the next two years? Then, we can begin to have children, and when the last child starts first grade, you can go back to college and finish your degree in chemistry. I promise, Patty." She enjoyed her chemistry classes, and it would be very disappointing and a great sacrifice for her.

This was our first major decision where that outcome could greatly impact our future together. Would she say, "No, I'm not willing to make that sacrifice," or would she say, "yes." Her answer? "Honey, we are a team, and if I need to drop out of college, get a job and support us, then I'll do it." That's what she did, and I graduated on schedule.

It was time for Patty to finish her education when our fourth child, Laura, entered first grade. "Sweetheart," I said, "If I were to die at an early age, and you didn't want to remarry, where would you get a job as a chemist in Pueblo, Colorado? Don't you think you should change your major from your first love, chemistry, to some other major?" Again, her answer would greatly impact our lives together and our future ministry for Christ. She replied, "Well, my second love of study would be childhood education. We are a team; I'll do it." She received her master's degree in Childhood Education from the University of Colorado in Colorado Springs in 1964.

The third major decision that shows my Love's support of me—as her husband—and our marriage, occurred after the death of our fifth child, Pamela. One morning about 10:30 a.m., Patty took nine-month old Pamela to the doctor. We stood by her little bed in Corwin Hospital and held her as she drew her last breath. This was a tragic, devastating time and life-changing event for us. I thought, "Maybe if I had been more attentive and taken Pamela to the doctor sooner, perhaps she would have lived." This thinking caused me great guilt, and I went into a deep, devastating depression. Again, my sweetheart, my support, stood by me as we contemplated life-changing decisions. During that depression, thoughts would come back to me of that morning.

Many years before, when World War II was raging, I was a young, eighteen-year-old Marine. We were about to land on an island in the South Pacific, and I thought perhaps I would die in a few minutes. I had been a believer in Christ since age eight, although

I had never been discipled. I made a vow to the Lord and told Him, "If you bring me through this war safely, I'll serve You when I get back home." He answered my prayer, but I didn't fulfill my vow. Was my daughter Pamela's death a reminder of my unfulfilled vow? I thought so. It was at that time that the Lord sent a devoted man of God, Ron Chadwick, to disciple me. After just eighteen months of loving discipleship, Ron moved to Kansas City, but my life had been changed forever.

The fourth major decision as a couple was upon us. One day I said to my beloved wife, "Baby Doll, I think the Lord is calling us into full-time ministry; what would you think of that?" Her answer? "What would that entail?" I replied, "Well, I would be asking you to give up our beautiful home in the Colorado countryside, leave all your friends and loved ones, move to Dallas to attend seminary where you will look at the back of my head for four years as I study for my master's degree in theology." Her reply was encouraging. She said, "I have already told the Lord I would go with you any place He wants to take you. I thought it would probably be a grass hut in New Guinea. Dallas would be much better than that." What a precious, godly wife.

We depleted our savings while we were at seminary. The fifth decision came quickly as Patty came to the rescue by teaching sixth grade in Mesquite.

After graduation, by our Lord's grace, we planted a new church in Denton, Texas called Denton Bible Church. We started with mainly college students who had no money. Mature adults with jobs were slow to come, and that meant a meager salary for us. "I'll go back to work," Patty said. "We're a team." For the past forty years, Patty had been a faithful wife, and once again she came to the rescue by working as a teacher at Trinity Christian Academy for the first nine years of the church. If she had not done that, we could not have remained at DBC.

Lastly, when we were in our sixties, Tommy took over as senior pastor. We hadn't yet developed a missions department at Denton Bible Church. Patty and I were in good health, and we wanted to finish strong. I asked Patty, "Would you be willing to travel to many different countries and help me? Patty, it will be difficult; jet lag, sleepless nights, and food and water that might kill us or make us very sick. Planes might crash; perhaps we will die together. We might face possible terrorist attacks, and many other dangers." Patty's response? "Let's go for it. God will be with us." We traveled internationally from age sixty-two to seventy-five.

I couldn't have asked for a more wonderful wife. She was all that my heart ever desired. "Thank you, Lord, and thank you, my sweetheart! Thank you, Sweetheart, for being a faithful and vital player on our team until your death separated us. I'll see you again soon, when by His grace, I will have done all He has planned for me and calls me home. Knowing that you will be there makes it easy for me to go home."

Mel read the following poem at Patty's memorial service on June 26, 2017:

> "Patty Lou, you have gone first, and I remain to
>   walk the road alone.
> I will live in memory of the happy days we
>   have known.
> In spring I'll watch for roses red when by faith
>   lilacs bloom.
> And in early fall when brown leaves fall, I'll catch a
>   glimpse of you.
> Sweetheart, you have gone first, and I remain for
>   battles to be fought;
> Each thing you have touched along the way will be
>   a hollow spot.
> I'll hear your voice; I'll see your smile, and though
>   blind now I may grope,
> But memories of your helping hand will bore me on
>   with hope.
> Precious, you have gone first, and I remain to finish
>   with the scroll.
> No lengthening shadow shall creep in to make this
>   life seem droll.
> We've known so much happiness, and we've had
>   our cup of joy (for 70+ years).

But memories are one gift from God that death
    cannot destroy.
Sweetheart, you have gone first, and I remain, but
    one thing I would ask of you,
Walk slowly down that long, long path, for soon I'll
    follow you.
And I will want to know each step you take, that I
    may walk the same,
For some day down that lonely road, you will hear
    me call your name.
Patty Lou, I love you!"

(Poem by Albert K. Rowswell)

Chapter 24

A Challenge from Mel

*A word of encouragement from someone who has
surpassed the age of Caleb of old.
(Joshua 14:10)*

It is my hope that these memories of what God has done will be
used to spur on His people to greater efforts for our Lord before
whom we shall all stand and give an account for our time spent on
this earth.

There is a vast army of older people that have been told their
days of usefulness are over. But look about you, my brothers and
sisters. There are untold numbers of younger evangelicals in their
teens and twenties who have never had a godly mom or dad to learn
from, to spend time with, and to be challenged with living a lifestyle
pleasing to their Lord. Take the initiative; ask our Lord to lead you
to someone that you can befriend in the name of Christ. "Care for
one another" (1 Corinthians 12:25).

If the pollsters are right, and I don't doubt them, there are large
numbers of Christians who have been redeemed from messed up
lives such as divorce, alcoholism, and so forth. Many of you think
you cannot be used in the Lord's service. Remember that when
Stephen, the first Christian martyr, was being stoned to death, the
murderers laid their coats at the feet of Saul of Tarsus (Acts 7:58)
who later became the Apostle Paul. If God can forgive someone who
had participated in murder and use him like He did Paul, He can use

you. Do as this converted murderer Paul said and did, "But one thing I do: Forgetting what is behind and straining toward what is ahead" (Philippians 3:13b). Get over the past. It is gone. It is forgiven. Go for broke in His service.

Next, to those of you in your successful careers who feel God is calling you to serve Him full-time but think it would be insanity to give it all up. That's how I thought at one time, but God was playing the role of the "The Hound of Heaven," and eventually He caught me about five years from retirement at age forty-eight. With my sweetheart's full support and blessings, we gave it all up. Of course, you don't have to do what God called me to do. Perhaps God is calling you to be faithful right where you are. Great – go for it.

To those of you who go to church but are not involved in ministry for Christ: you aren't really living. God has a wonderful plan for your life. "The thief comes only to steal and kill and destroy; I came that they may have life and have it abundantly" (John 10:10). May I encourage you to get trained to minister using your spiritual gift. We all have one (1 Corinthians 7:7). May our Lord bless you greatly.

Finally, to the faithful pastors who are sometimes overworked, underpaid, and often receive little appreciation, may I challenge you to train or equip your lay people to do ministry using their spiritual gifts to help you (Ephesians 4:11-12). This is God's will, and the only way you can keep from working yourself into exhaustion. May our Lord bless and comfort you.

Here is a good principle to live by, quoted from my beloved Professor Gene Getz' *Life Essentials Study Bible*: "If we are to discover true meaning and fulfillment in life, now and eternally, we must come to God through faith in the Lord Jesus Christ," and serve Him faithfully and to the max!

Anything that has been accomplished in and through my life was made possible only through the grace of our Lord Jesus Christ. I give Him all the glory and praise!

Mel Sumrall
Pastor (Emeritus)
Denton Bible Church

Appendices

<u>List of countries Mel and Patty have visited</u>

Holland
Scotland
Israel
Greece
Ancient Corinth
Ephesus (Turkey)
Egypt
England
France
Switzerland
Romania
Ukraine
Russia
Siberia
China
India
Nepal
Bangladesh
Thailand

Philippines
Italy
Latvia
Burma
Kenya
Argentina
Brazil
Chile
Columbia
Central America
Indonesia
Malaysia
Tibet
Solomon Islands
Australia
New Zealand
Ecuador
Macedonia
Spain

South Korea
Cambodia
Vietnam
Guam
Panama
Republic of Georgia
Venezuela
Austria
Kuwait
Mongolia
Hong Kong
Germany
Mexico
Taiwan
Japan
Singapore

Ministries at Denton
Bible Church

Abortion Recovery
Abuse Recovery
Adult Bible Fellowship
Ambassadors (help newcomers)
American Heritage Girls
Awana
Beauty for Ashes (infertility/
    miscarriage)
Bereavement & Funerals
Bereavement Meal Team
Bible Training Center for
    Leaders (women)
Bible Training Center for
    Pastors (men)
Buddy for Me (special needs)
Cancer Support Group
Career Transitions Ministry
Cattle Ministry
Children's Ministry
Christian Service Brigade
ChurchLife Ministry
Cornerstone (singles over 40)
Counseling Ministry
DBC Cares (meals, support for
    illness, death)
DBC en Espanol
DBCU (college)
DBSM (Jr. high & high
    school students)
Deaf Ministry
Denton Bible Choir
Denton County Home
    School Assn.
Divorce Care

Family Grace Group
    (support for families of
    mental illness)
Financial Ministry
Gardening Ministry
Grace Recovery (alcohol/drug
    support group)
GriefShare
Habitat for Humanity
Impact (women's mento-
    ring program)
Incarcerated Ministry
International Student Ministry
Kids Clubs
Kids Praise Camp
Kids Praise Choir
Lay Institute
Living Hope (support for
    those struggling with
    homosexuality)
Living Water (support for
    those struggling with
    depression/anxiety)
Media Ministry
Men's Discipleship
Men's Ministry – REAL Men
Men's Morning Bible Study
Men's Redemption Group
Mercy Heart (support for
    families of incarcerated)
Middle School Choir
Military Prayer
Military Life (caring for mili-
    tary & families)
Missionary Training
Missions Serve International

Missions & You (women's
    missions)
MOMS
Moms in Prayer International
Music Ministry
Navigators 2:7 (Discipleship
    training)
Operation Christmas Child
    (Samaritan's Purse)
Orchestra
Orphan Care
Parenting Ministry
Parking Ministry
Pastoral Care & Hospital
    Visitation
Practicing Positive Parenting
Prayer Chain
Prayer Counselors
Prayer Shawl Ministry
Premarital Counseling
Preschool Ministry
Print Media
Reengage Ministry (marriage)
Rise Adults (special needs)
Rise Jr.
Rise Tweens
Safe Harbor Advocacy (helping
    women in crisis)
SeniorLife (older adults)
SeniorLife Singles
Short-Term Missions
Single Women &
    Widows Ministry
Spanish Sunday Bible
    Fellowship
Spanish Translation
Sportsworld

Starting Point
Step Family Ministry
Student Choir
Student Ministries
Sweat Team (repairs, cleanup to
    those in need)
Tapestry (Single women)
Titus 2 International
Trail Life USA
Twice as Nice Resale Shop
    (benefits Woman to Woman
    Pregnancy Center)
Unshackled (men struggling
    with past as ex-convicts)
Vacation Bible School
Vision Ministries (food &
    clothing for needy)
Wall of Prayer (prayer
    for Jr. High & High
    School students)
Wedding Ministry
Woman to Woman
    Pregnancy Resource
Women Serving God (Teacher
    & leadership training)
Women's Ministry
WorldLife (outreach to interna-
    tional students)
Young Guns (9 month
    discipleship program for
    young men)
Young Adults
Young Singles

Missionaries
  23 SERVE missionaries
  52 Affiliated/Endorsed missionaries
  20 National Partners (live overseas and help partners)

A Free Gift

Dear Friend,

It is possible Mel could have been president of CF&I if he had continued with the company. Mel has no regrets about leaving a skyrocketing career to pursue a relationship with the Creator of the universe with all his heart, mind, and strength. He traded power, material possessions, and a comfortable lifestyle for love, peace and joy that only comes from trusting Jesus Christ as Lord and Savior.

If you find yourself with an empty, meaningless life despite the outward appearance of success, then you too can experience the same love, peace and joy that Mel and billions of Christians through the ages have found. God offers the free gift of salvation through His Son, Jesus Christ. Here is the gospel explained.

Gospel means "good news." According to the Bible, then, the Gospel is the good news about salvation, or about being saved.

> **Romans 5:8** But God demonstrates his own love for us, in that while we were still sinners, Christ died for us.

According to <u>Romans 5:8</u>, God demonstrated His love for us through the death of His Son. Why did Christ have to die for us? Because Scripture declares all men to be sinful. To "sin" means to miss the mark. The Bible declares "all have sinned and fall short of the glory (the perfect holiness) of God" (<u>Rom. 3:23</u>). In other words, our sin separates us from God who is perfect holiness (righteousness and justice) and God must therefore judge sinful man.

Scripture also teaches that no amount of human goodness, human works, human morality, or religious activity can gain acceptance with God or get anyone into heaven. The moral man, the religious man, and the immoral and non-religious are all in the same boat. They all fall short of God's perfect righteousness.

> **Ephesians 2:8-9** For by grace you are saved through faith, and this is not of yourselves, it is the gift of God; 9 it is not of works, so that no one can boast.

No amount of human goodness is as good as God. God is perfect righteousness. Because of this, Habakkuk 1:13 tells us God cannot have fellowship with anyone who does not have perfect righteousness. To be accepted by God, we must be as good as God is. Before God, we all stand naked, helpless, and hopeless in ourselves. No amount of good living will get us to heaven or give us eternal life. What then is the solution?

God's Solution

God is not only perfect holiness (whose holy character we can never attain to on our own or by our works of righteousness) but He is also perfect love and full of grace and mercy. Because of His love and grace, He has not left us without hope and a solution.

> **Romans 5:8** But God demonstrates his own love for us, in that while we were still sinners, Christ died for us.

This is the good news of the Bible, the message of the gospel. It's the message of the gift of God's own Son who became man (the God-man), lived a sinless life, died on the cross for our sin, and was raised from the grave proving both the fact He is God's Son and the value of His death for us as our substitute.

Because of what Jesus Christ accomplished for us on the cross, the Bible states "He that has the Son has life." We can receive the

Son, Jesus Christ, as our Savior by personal faith, by trusting in the person of Christ and His death for our sins.

> **John 1:12** But to all who have received him–those who believe in his name–he has given the right to become God's children

> **John 3:16-18** For this is the way God loved the world: he gave his one and only Son that everyone who believes in him should not perish but have eternal life. 17 For God did not send his Son into the world to condemn the world, but that the world should be saved through him. 18 The one who believes in Him is not condemned. The one who does not believe has been condemned already, because he has not believed in the name of the one and only Son of God.

This means we must each come to God the same way: (1) as a sinner who recognizes his sinfulness, (2) realizes no human works can result in salvation, and (3) relies totally on Christ alone by faith alone for our salvation.

If you would like to receive and trust Christ as your personal Savior, you can do so by praying a simple prayer acknowledging your sinfulness, accepting His forgiveness and putting your faith in Christ for your salvation.

If you prayed to trust Christ as your Savior, contact Denton Bible Church for free materials on what to do next.

Denton Bible Church
Address: 2300 E University Dr, Denton, TX 76209
Phone: (940) 297-6700
Website: http://dentonbible.org

Bibliography

1. Dictionary of American History. The Gale Group, Inc. 2003. "Great Depression facts, information, pictures." Accessed April 12, 2017. https: www.encyclopedia.com/history/united-states-and-canada/us-history/great-depression.

2. 30 Dust Bowl Facts: U.S. History for Kids. http://www.american-historama.org/1929-1945-depression-ww2-era/dust-bowl.htm. Accessed April 12, 2017.

3. Youth work 1930's – The Economy and Youth. http://theyouthinthe 1930s.weebly.com/youth-work-1930s.html. Accessed April 12, 2017.

4. V-J Day. Article. http://www.history.com/topics/world-war-ii/v-j-day. Accessed May 4, 2017.

5. Serviceman's Readjustment Act (1944). https://www.ourdocuments.gov/doc.php?flash=true&doc=76. Accessed May 6, 2017.

Connie Cohn is blessed with son and daughter-in-law, Dale and Allison who have given her three precious grandkids, Jacob, Josh and Joy. Connie is passionate about encouraging women to follow hard after Christ. She is a graduate of Dallas Theological Seminary. Connie lives in Denton, Texas with her two cats, George and Mewler.

CPSIA information can be obtained
at www.ICGtesting.com
Printed in the USA
FSHW01n0026010918